CLYDE BUILT SHIPS

CLYDE BUILT SHIPS

JAMES A. POTTINGER

Dedicated to my grandaughter and shining light,
Phoebe India Pottinger

Cover Illustrations. Front: Bamora (II) by Harland and Wolff, Glasgow, 1960. (Chris Howell) *Back*: *Queen Elizabeth* by John Brown, Clydebank, 1938. (Author)

First published 2013

The History Press
The Mill, Brimscombe Port
Stroud, Gloucestershire, GL5 2QG
www.thehistorypress.co.uk

British Library Cataloguing in Publication Data.
A catalogue record for this book is available from the British Library.

ISBN 978 0 7524 8999 5

Typesetting and origination by The History Press
Printed in Great Britain

Contents

Acknowledgements

Information has necessarily been culled from a wide variety of sources in print and various registers from databases and other records, including the invaluable Clyde-built Database on the www.clydesite.co.uk website. To the many compilers of this database and all who have provided photos and data I offer my grateful thanks, all the while accepting full responsibility for any errors, which are my own.

Again offering apologies to my long-suffering spouse for books, papers, photographs etc. scattered widely, and not always neatly, during the gestation of this, another maritime volume.

Note regarding photo source attribution:
'Author' signifies my own negatives
'Author's collection' is used for those of unknown origin
The name of the owner of the original negative is used where known
Negative originator in current collection of named custodian is used if known

Machinery abbreviations, prefixed with number of screws:

1Sc-MV	Single screw motor
1Sc-ST	Single screw steam turbine
1Sc-2Cyl	Single screw steam compound reciprocating
1Sc-T3Cyl	Single screw steam triple expansion reciprocating
1Sc-4TCyl	Single screw 4-cylinder triple expansion
1Sc-QCyl	Single screw 4-cylinder quadruple expansion
1Sc-STE	Steam turbine electric steam ship
1Sc-DEMV	Diesel electric motor vessel
2Sc-VS	Two Voith-Schneider propellers
PS	Steam paddle
DEP	Diesel electric paddle
1Sc-CODOG	Single screw combined diesel or gas turbine
1Sc-COGOG	Single screw combined gas or gas turbine

1Sc-COSAG	Combined steam and gas turbine
1Sc-FPGT	Single screw free piston gas turbine
1Sc-Osc	Single screw oscillating

Note: The first date is that of launch where known. The name is as shown in the illustrations.

Introduction

Whilst shipbuilding and engineering on the River Clyde had their origins in the very earliest days of these industries' development, the Clyde has long specialised in the manufacture of a wide range of these applications afloat. Indeed, it would be difficult to think of any class of seagoing vessel that has not at one time been launched into the waters of the Clyde; many of these vessels have even been pioneers in their own particular field. Possibly no other shipbuilding centre has ever covered such a wide spectrum of marine craft, from the humble steam puffer through to the sailing ship, to the most sophisticated ocean passenger liner and surface and underwater warship, with a multitude of varieties in between which include oil and gas tankers, cable ships, drill ships, dredgers, tugs, coastal paddle and screw passenger vessels, yachts, fishing boats, ferries and excursion vessels.

Some individual establishments could turn out almost the whole range, from large passenger liners to sophisticated cargo passenger ships and all types of warships. One shipyard in particular – Scotts' of Greenock – at different times built and engined most of the above categories.

One example included shows the dilemma facing Clyde builders in trying to cater successfully for such a wide range of ships. The photograph in question shows the passenger cargo ship *Centaur* and the large tanker *British Mariner* fitting out simultaneously at John Brown at Clydebank. The more specialist design of the former exhibits a more complex hull shape and a high level of fitting-out expertise; however, to profitably progress construction of the latter, the fast and efficient throughput of steel fabrication was paramount.

There was, however, a degree of specialisation practised by some builders, for example Lobnitz – later Simons-Lobnitz – predominated in the field of dredging. Others such as Scott & Sons, Bowling, Ferguson Bros and James Lamont of Port Glasgow concentrated on tugs, coasters and other small craft. Lithgows tended to concentrate, in the early days, on large standard cargo-carrying sailing ships, and later general cargo ships and tramps but with some exceptions.

The Clyde's worldwide predominance was due to a number of factors, amongst which were the location and access to ready supplies of coal and minerals suitable for the production of iron ore and subsequent manufacture of iron and then later steel, an increase in the population of readily available labour and an education system which laid great store on the more practical applications of science, chemistry and mechanics.

However, many of the innovators in the early advances of marine engineering and shipbuilding relied on their intuitive and innate skills and not solely on advanced learning.

It is perhaps not widely known but many of the early iron- and steel-powered ships were the result of the engineers expanding their activities to take advantage of the advances in marine engineering, providing an obvious outlet for their pioneering developments in steam power and applying these to marine propulsion. This is exemplified by the fact that the hulls of many early vessels ordered from engineers were subcontracted to shipbuilders.

The various reasons for the demise of the Clyde shipbuilding and engineering industry, as it was, have been postulated widely and extensively. It is suffice to say that in addition to the effect of economic changes worldwide and the revolution in sea transport, some of that responsibility can justifiably be laid at the door of the owners, management and labour force, not forgetting the direction and intent of the policies of the governments of the day.

Given the wide scope of construction and numbers of completions, the selection of photographs here does not entirely offer a fair representation of the diverse types of Clyde-built vessels, but it is hoped the following will be of interest and give a flavour of when the Clyde was a prime shipbuilding and engineering centre. I have also included some illustrations which feature realistic models built to model plans I have drawn.

Within the constraints of the chosen published format, the captions are somewhat brief, but it is hoped that the ensuing pages will illustrate the immense variety of vessels indicative of the varied products of the River Clyde.

James A. Pottinger, 2013

1

Passenger and Cargo Liners

The major shipyards on the Clyde all built passenger and cargo liners at one time, and in some cases the connection between the shipowner and builder was in the form of a shareholding or other long-standing link, often due to the relationship between the principals of each. These include Cunard and John Brown, P&O and Cairds at Greenock, British India Steam Navigation Co. (BI) and Barclay Curle, and Connells and the Ben Line. The connection between Scotts' and Swire and Alfred Holt embodied financial interests and also a favoured shipbuilder, and was probably the longest continuous association.

The passenger liners and cargo ships have been grouped together in this chapter because many of the passenger ships shown all carried some cargo, and many of the cargo ships had accommodation for a number of passengers, thus blurring any definitive categorisation.

1Sc-MV **ANSHUN (I)**

27/10/1930: Scotts' of Greenock to China Navigation Co., yard no. 552. 1939: As Admiralty RAN *Anshun Y1*; 1941: Damaged by Japanese aircraft at Manila Bay; 1942: Shelled and sunk at Milne Bay by Japanese warships. 06/1944: Salved, renamed *Culcairn*. 1964: As livestock carrier *Lombok*. 1966: Fire damaged at Surabaya, scrapped at Hong Kong in July. (A. Duncan, *Ships in Focus*)

1Sc-MV **ARHON**

14/09/1973: Scotstoun Marine Ltd, Glasgow, yard no. 129C, as *Harfleur* (II) for J. & C. Harrison. With *Harfleet*, yard no. 125 at these builders, she was the last deep-sea ship in the owners' fleet. Passed through numerous owners with the following names: *Chi Trust* (1979); *Arhon* (1986). 18/11/1997: Arrived Alang, India, for scrapping. (Chris Howell)

1Sc-T3Cyl **BAMORA (I)**

07/04/1914: Barclay Curle & Co., Glasgow, yard no. 508, for BI; last of the B class and designed for the Bombay–Basra service. New, she joined the Indian Expeditionary Force serving until October 1919. Served as an armament stores ship from January 1942. 30/06/1950: Sold to the Indian Steel Syndicate for scrapping at Bombay. (P&O)

1Sc-ST **BENLOYAL (III)**
03/10/1958: Charles Connell & Co., Scotstoun, yard no. 489, for William Thomson. One of the first 20-knot ships in the British Merchant Navy; designed for the UK–Singapore–Hong Kong service, confirmed Ben Line as strong competitors to Blue Funnel. 06/06/1978: At Inchon for scrapping which began at Busan on 5 January 1979. (Ben Line)

1Sc-ST **BENREOCH (III)**
11/08/1952: Charles Connell & Co., Glasgow, yard no. 472, for Ben Line Steamers; one of the improved 17- to 18-knot ships beginning with the *Benvrackie* (V). 05/1976: Sold to Tudis Navigation Piraeus, renamed *Tudis*. 16/03/1979: Arrived at Kaohsiung for scrapping by Gi Yuen Steel Enterprise Ltd. (Ben Line)

2Sc-MV **CALEDONIA STAR**
29/07/1942: Greenock Dockyard, yard no. 451 *Empire Wisdom*, with twin triple expansion and Bauer Wach exhaust turbines for MOWT, Clan Line managers. 1944: Blue Star appointed managers. 19/09/1946: Renamed *Royal Star* (III). 1961: Re-engined with diesels, renamed *Caledonia Star*. 1971: To Ta Yung Steel Co., Taiwan. 09/12/1971: At Kaohsiung, scrapping began on 1 January 1972. (A. Duncan, *Ships in Focus*)

1Sc-MV **CAPE HAWKE**
21/05/1940: Lithgows Ltd, Port Glasgow, yard no. 930, for Cape York Motorship Co. Ltd (Lyle Shipping Co. Ltd). 1963: To Kalliopi Compania Naviera S.A., Panama, renamed *Kalliopi*; later that year to Compania Naviera Skaros S.A., Panama, renamed *Roy*. 31/03/1967: Broke crankshaft and towed to Honolulu, then Okohama; uneconomic to repair. 28/08/1977: Sold, towed to Mihara for scrapping. (A. Duncan, *Ships in Focus*)

1Sc-MV **CAPE ORTEGAL (III)**
20/11/1975: Govan Shipbuilders, yard no. 215, for Lyle Motorship Co. One of the Cardiff class, as the first had been for William Reardon Smith & Sons; 31 were completed between 1970 and 1981. Sold in 1982, she had following names: *Kilmun* (1982); *Esperanza* (1986); *Delena I* (1989); *Vizcaya* (1992); *Andaxios* (1992). 02/08/2001: Arrived in Mumbai for scrapping. (Chris Howell)

3Sc-ST **CARMANIA**
21/02/1905: John Brown, Clydebank, yard no. 366, for Cunard Steamship Co. First Cunard turbine ship, and was intended as a comparison with the quadruple-reciprocating-engined *Caronia*. Taken as Armed Merchant Cruiser (AMC) in WWI. 14/09/1914: Sank German armed cruiser *Cap Trafalgar* off South American coast. 22/04/1932: Arrived for scrapping at Blyth. (Author's collection)

2Sc-ST **CASTEL FELICE**
27/08/1930: Alexander Stephen & Sons Ltd, Glasgow, yard no. 529, for BI as *Kenya* (I). 04/1940: Taken by Royal Navy as *Hydra*, renamed *Keren*, carrying 24 landing craft. 03/04/1946: Bought by MoT from RN. 1948: Laid up for two years, renamed *Kenya*, *Keren* and then *Kenya*. 05/1949: To Vlasov Group, rebuilt at Genoa for Australian emigrant trade as *Castel Felice*. 15/08/1970: On fire at Southampton. 01/1971: Scrapping at Kaohsiung. (Malcolm Cranfield)

2Sc-MV **CENTAUR (III)**
20/06/1963: John Brown, Clydebank, yard no. 722, for Alfred Holt. Designed for 190 passengers and 4,500 sheep or 700 cattle, for Singapore–Fremantle trade, able to take the ground. 1982: Chartered to St Helena Shipping Co. to replace their requisitioned *St Helena* during the Falklands War. 1985: Sold to China as *Hai Long*, *Hai Da* in 1986. 2006: Scrapped. (Author)

1Sc-MV **CHANGSHA (IV)**
02/11/1948: Scotts' of Greenock, yard no. 645, for China Navigation Co.; the first of two ships for Australian service. 26/09/1959: Blown ashore at Nagoya and refloated six months later. 06/1959: Sold to Pacific International Lines (Pte), Singapore, renamed *Kota Panjang* (I). 16/06/1981: Arrived at Gadani Beach for scrapping. (Dr George S. Wilson)

1Sc-ST **CHIRRIPO**
26/08/1957: Alexander Stephen & Sons Ltd, Glasgow, yard no. 658, for Elders & Fyffes. One of four fast fruit ships. 1969: Sold to Empreso Hondureña de Vapor, Honduras, and renamed *Olancho*. 1972: To Newport Shipping Co., Greece, and renamed *Mardina Exporter*. 06/06/1974: Arrived at Kaohsiung for scrapping. (Malcolm Cranfield)

1Sc-ST **CITY OF AGRA**
02/10/1936: William Denny & Bros, Dumbarton, yard no. 1289, for Ellerman Lines. A unique profile in the fleet with a long centre castle which incorporated hatch no. 3 in front of the bridge and was surprisingly fitted with coal-fired boilers. Her longevity saw service until arrival at Bilbao on 17 May 1965 for scrapping. (Malcolm Cranfield)

2Sc-T3Cyl + Exh. Turbine **CLAN BUCHANAN (III)**
21/12/1937: Greenock Dockyard, yard no. 431, for Clan Line Steamers. 05/04/1940: Requisitioned by the government. 28/04/1941: Sunk by German armed raider *Pinguin* (Schiff no. 33) off the Maldives. From a crew of 119, at least 106 survivors were lost when the raider was sunk by HMS *Cornwall* on 9 May 1941. (Clan Line)

1Sc-MV **CLAN GRANT (IV)**
22/12/1961: Greenock Dockyard, yard no. 499, for Clan Line Steamers. One of a group of seven F and G class, fitted with Sulzers instead of Doxfords; Fs were built by Swan Hunter and the Gs by Greenock Dockyard. 12/1980: To Venables Steamship S.A., Panama, renamed *Enriqueta*. 15/01/1958: Arrived in China for scrapping. (Malcolm Cranfield)

2Sc-ST **CLAN MACTAVISH (III)**
02/03/1949: Greenock Dockyard, yard no. 470, for Clan Line Steamers; only sister to *Clan Mactaggart*. At 125 tons, derricks were the heaviest in the fleet at that time; first ships in the fleet to have white extending down the hull. 22/10/1971: At Whampoa only 22 years old for scrapping, steam turbines making her uneconomic. (Malcolm Cranfield)

2Sc-MV **CLAN MACDONALD (IV)**
15/08/1939: Greenock Dockyard, yard no. 436, for Clan Line Steamers. 01/1941: Commodore ship in convoy UK–Piraeus, with numerous air attacks, then to Brisbane for meat to UK. 10/1941: Made fast run from Malta to Gibraltar with 11 passengers. 14/03/1966: Rescued nine survivors from the *World Liberty-Mosli* collision. 06/08/1970: Arrived at Shanghai for scrapping. (Author's collection)

1Sc-MV **CLAN MALCOLM (II)**
29/04/1957: Greenock Dockyard, yard no. 490, for Clan Line Steamers. Similar profile to steamers *Clan Ross* and *Clan Robertson* but without funnel cowl and with added samson posts on poop; was cadet ship in 1960s. 1979: To Bective Shipping Co., Panama, with *Clan Menzies*, renamed *Trinity Fair*. 25/05/1979: Left Bangkok for Shanghai for scrapping. (Author)

2Sc-ST **CORFU**
20/05/1931: Alexander Stephen & Sons Ltd, Glasgow, yard no. 534, for P&O. 14/09/1939: For conversion to AMC by Harland and Wolff, after funnel removed and armed. 17/02/1944: To owners as a troopship, converted at Mobile. 22/01/1949: In commercial service. 24/03/1961: Sold, renamed *Corfu Maru*. 17/10/1961: Scrapping at Osaka. (A. Duncan, *Ships in Focus*)

2Sc-MV **DEVONIA**
20/12/1938: Fairfield, Govan, yard no. 670, as troopship *Devonshire* (I) for Bibby Line Ltd. To same builders in April 1953 for refit. 17/01/1962: Sold to BI, refitted by Barclay Curle, renamed *Devonia* and made 110 educational cruises. 15/12/1967: To S.A. Cantiere Navale de Santa Maria of Genoa, began scrapping at Spezia in January 1968. (BI)

2Sc-MV **DOMALA**
21/12/1920: Barclay Curle & Co., Glasgow, yard no. 579, for BI. 23/05/1922: Launched as *Magvana*. 02/02/1940: Bombed off Isle of Wight and set on fire; 108 lives lost; hulk brought to Southampton. Reconstructed as *Empire Attendant*. 15/07/1942: Torpedoed by *U-582* SW off Canary Islands, 50 crew and 9 gunners lost. (A. Duncan, *Ships in Focus*)

1Sc-MV **EGORI (II)**
12/06/1956: Scotts' of Greenock, yard no. 673, for Elder Dempster; Scotts' built and installed first turbocharged Doxford diesel. 06/09/1978: Sold to Ali Khalifa Mirchandani Shipping Co., Kuwait, and renamed *Azza*. 1979: To Ali Navigation Co., Kuwait, then sold to Li Chong Iron Works Co. Ltd for scrapping. 09/10/1979: Arrived at Kaohsiung. (A. Duncan, *Ships in Focus*)

2Sc-ST **ETHIOPIA (III)**
15/12/1921: William Denny & Bros, Dumbarton, yard no. 1040, for BI. Coal or oil firing. Intended for Calcutta–Singapore run. Worked as a personnel ship and trooper in WWII. 20/05/1940: Sold for Rs 625,000 with *Vita* (1914) to Tulsiram Bhagwandas of Calcutta for scrapping at Bombay. (A. Duncan, *Ships in Focus*)

2Sc-MV **EURYBATES**
28/10/1927: Scotts' of Greenock, yard no. 533, for Alfred Holt. Scott-Still combined steam/diesel engines, where exhaust heat from the diesels used to steam for the steam part of engines; was efficient, but increasing maintenance costs led to conversion to pure diesel provided by Harland and Wolff in 1948. 15/07/1958: To Ghent for scrapping. (A. Duncan, *Ships in Focus*)

2Sc-ST **FAIRSTAR**
15/12/1955: Fairfield, yard no. 775, as *Oxfordshire* – troopship for Bibby Line Ltd. After MoD contract was chartered by Fairline Shipping Corp. 20/05/1963: Wilton-Fijenoord BV converted to passenger/cruise liner. 03/1964: Bought by Fairstar Shipping Corp., renamed *Fairstar*. 04/1964: Conversion completed by Harland and Wolff at Southampton. 01/09/1988: Bought by P&O, now managers. 11/02/1997: Sold to Rugby Enterprises for scrapping. 10/04/1997: Arrived at Alang. (Author's collection)

1Sc-MV **FOURAH BAY**
07/09/1961: Scotts' of Greenock, yard no. 689, for Elder Dempster. 05/01/1958: To Xoces Ltd, Bermuda, renamed *Magda Josefina*. 06/1980: To Faith Shipping Co. S.A., Panama, renamed *Alexander's Faith*. 13/08/1982: Laid up at Piraeus. 05/10/1983: To Lemina Maritime Co. Ltd, Cyprus, renamed *Lemina*. 03/03/1983: Sold for scrapping at Gadani Beach. (Malcolm Cranfield)

2Sc-MV **GLENROY**
15/08/1938: Scotts' of Greenock, yard no. 571, for Glen Line. 10/1939: Requisitioned as Fleet Supply Ship. 10/06/1940: Taken for conversion to Landing Ship (Infantry) Large. 21/06/1946: To owners and returned to commercial service. 09/1966: To Ataka & Co., Japan, resold and started demolition on 02/11/1966 by Tarumoto Sangyo K.K. at Kure. (A. Duncan, *Ships in Focus*)

1Sc-MV **GLORY SKY**
14/05/1971: Upper Clyde Shipbuilders Ltd, Govan, yard no. 114, for Cardigan Shipping Co. Ltd, as *Norse Marshal*. Carried the following names after being sold: *Astro Carrier* (1985–87); *Carrie* (1987–89); *Glory Sky* (1989–93); *Fotoni* (1993–94); *Paris* (1994–95). 04/01/1995: As *Paris* struck breakwater at Constantza in a storm and wrecked; all 27 crew lost. (Chris Howell)

1Sc-T3Cyl **HAKAN**
14/02/1944: Lithgows Ltd, Port Glasgow, yard no. 991, for Crest Shipping Co. Ltd (Overseas Navigation Trust Ltd, London) as *Lloydcrest*. 1958: Renamed *Sinop*. 1963: Renamed *Hakan*. 12/01/1979: Collided with and sank *Dragon*, ex-*Mitera Eirini*, ex-*St Magnus*, ex-*City Of Durham*, in Bosphorus; seen laid up at Sariyer with bow damage. 10/1979: Scrapped at Aliağa, Turkey. (Malcolm Cranfield)

2Sc-ST **HANSEATIC**
17/12/1929: Fairfield, Govan, yard no. 634, as *Empress of Japan*. 26/11/1942: Renamed *Empress of Scotland*. 13/01/1958: To Hamburg-Atlantic Line. 22/01/1958: Converted and renamed *Hanseatic*; 07/09/1966: Caught fire at New York; towed to Hamburg. 11/06/1966: To Eckhardt & Co., Hamburg, for scrap. (A. Duncan, *Ships in Focus*)

2Sc-ST **HOMELAND**
22/12/1904: Alexander Stephen & Sons Ltd, Linthouse, yard no. 405, as *Virginian* for Allan Line. 1920: As *Drottningholm* of Swedish American. 1948: To Home Lines, renamed *Brasil*. 01/06/1951: Renamed *Homeland*. 1955: Sold for scrapping at Trieste. Over 50 years she had served four owners with four names, and was the second turbine ship on the North Atlantic. (A. Duncan, *Ships in Focus*)

1Sc-T3Cyl **HUNAN (II)**
01/11/1932: Scotts' of Greenock, yard no. 555, for China Navigation Co., the first of seven sister ships. In 1941 was intercepted by Japanese warships and Chinese cargo confiscated; was also attacked by armed junks near Hong Kong in 1951. 13/01/1962: At Hong Kong for scrapping. This model was built by John Mackay to the author's model plan. (Author's collection)

1Sc-MV **IBERIC**
22/11/1960: Alexander Stephen & Sons Ltd, yard no. 671, for Shaw Savill – their first ship for these owners since 1921, and the only one built on the Clyde of a similar quartet. 28/05/1969: Laid up in River Blackwater. 1976: To Royal Mail management and renamed *Deseado.* 20/05/1983: Arrived at Chittagong as *San George* for scrapping. (Author)

1Sc-ST **KENUTA**
22/05/1950: Greenock Dockyard, yard no. 473, for Pacific Steam Navigation Co. Ltd. One of a quartet; the others were *Flamenco* and *Potosi*, and *Cotopaxi* by William Denny of basically a Clan Line design. 24/06/1971: Scrapped at Tamise, Belgium. (Malcolm Cranfield)

1Sc-MV **LACANDON**
18/05/1970: Upper Clyde Shipbuilders, yard no. 843G, as *Victoria City* for William Reardon Smith & Sons. One of first four of the 26,000 class built for this owner. Passed through several owners and names: *Lacandon* (1983); *Singa Swan* (1988); *Monolima* (1993), and scrapped under that name. 19/02/1966: Scrapping at Kakinada, India. (Chris Howell)

1Sc-MV **LORD GLADSTONE**
29/02/1959: Scotts' of Greenock, yard no. 680, a large tramp ship for Geo. Nicolaou Ltd. Renamed as: *N. Zografia* (1969); *Constantinos T* (1975); *Capetan Costis* (1978); *Stylani* then *Maldive Privilege* (1981); *Dynasty Hura* (1984). 26/09/1984: Described as a hulk. Scrapped at Chittagong. (Malcolm Cranfield)

1Sc-ST **MAGDAPUR (I)**
17/11/1920: Lithgows Ltd, Port Glasgow, yard no. 730, for T. & J. Brocklebank. Seen as built, but as a result of the depressed state of the shipping industry and trading conditions, she was shortened by 35ft by Smith's Dock, Middlesbrough, in 1935; three other ships similarly altered. 10/09/1939: Mined and sunk off Aldeburgh. (A. Duncan, *Ships in Focus*)

1Sc-ST **MAHSEER (II)**
1948: William Hamilton & Co., Port Glasgow, yard no. 475, for T. & J. Brocklebank. Similar to *Matra*, with three Samson posts instead of a main mast, and *Manaar* having a single mast. At 508ft 5in overall, they were just within the limits of the locks of Kidderpore Dock, Calcutta. 06/1975: Arrived at Karachi for scrapping. (Author; model by Peter Bryant)

1Sc-TCyl **MAIHAR (I)**
16/04/1917: Russell & Co., Port Glasgow, yard no. 679, for T. & J. Brocklebank. Sister to *Mahsud*. 1956–57: Rebuilt by A. Stephen at Glasgow: oil-fired boilers, auxiliaries, accommodation, swimming pool, mainmast top discarded and four lifeboats on boat deck only. 1961: Sold to Eastbound Tankers Corp., Monrovia, and renamed *Capella*. 24/05/1962: Arrived at Hirao, Japan, for scrapping. (Malcolm Cranfield)

1Sc-ST **MANCHESTER REGIMENT**
16/10/1946: Blythswood Shipbuilding Co. Ltd, yard no. 84, for Manchester Liners. 1967: To Astro Tropico Compania Naviera S.A., Panama, and renamed *Azure Coast II*. 1970: To United Maritime Management Co., Singapore, and renamed *Pu Gor*. 22/12/1971: Arrived for scrapping at Kaohsiung. (Malcolm Cranfield)

1Sc-ST **MANIPUR (III)**
29/05/1945: William Hamilton & Co., Port Glasgow, yard no. 461, for T. & J. Brocklebank. First delivery after end of WWII. 12/1960: Tooth broke off main gear wheel leaving Newport SW (outward voyage) at reduced speed and with a wrecked diesel generator at Aden; replaced on return. 12/1966: To Hong Kong for scrapping. 06/01/1967: Arrived at Whampoa for scrapping. (Author)

1Sc-ST **MARGARET BOWATER**
14/09/1954: William Denny & Bros, Dumbarton, yard no. 1471, for Bowater Steamship Co. Ltd. First ship in this owner's fleet and intended to carry raw material from their mills in Canada, USA and Scandinavia. 1968: To Auxiliary Power Corp., renamed *John W. Hill*. 1970: To Jeronimo Corp., Monrovia, renamed *Grand State*. 06/1971: Scrapped at Kaohsiung, Taiwan. (Ken Cunnington, Roy Fenton)

1Sc-ST **MARTABAN (IV)**
06/09/1949: William Denny & Bros, Dumbarton, yard no. 1435, for British & Burmese Shipping Co. Ltd. 30/01/1952: To Elder Dempster. 1963: To China Merchants S.N., Taipei, renamed *Hai Ho*. 07/07/1971: At Kaohsiung, resold to Ken Hsieng Na Co., Taipei, renamed *Ken Ho 5*. Scrapped by Universal Steel Enterprises Corp. at Kaohsiung. (A. Duncan, *Ships in Focus*)

1Sc-FPGT **MORAR**
23/04/1958: Lithgows Ltd, Port Glasgow, yard no. 1113, for Denholms Ltd. Fitted with a pioneering geared gas turbine supplied by gas from three gasifiers. The high consumption costs incurred in a basic ore carrier militated against any repeats. 1967: Sold and renamed *Clari*, re-engined with diesel. 09/1979: Aground as *Mahoni* off Taiwan and broken up the following year. (Author's collection)

1Sc-MV **MYRMIDON (V)**
19/02/1980: Scotts' of Greenock, yard no. 751, for Ocean Transport & Trading Co. With sisters *Maron* (IV) and *Mentor* (III) they cost £36 million. The last merchant ship built by Scotts'. Had following names: *Capetown Carrier, Myrmidon, Bello Folawiyo, CMB Exporter, Merchant Promise, Lanka Amila, Merchant Promise* and finally *Tamamonta*. 16/01/2002: Arrived at Alang for scrapping. (Malcolm Cranfield)

1Sc-T3Cyl **NANCHANG (II)**
29/07/1922: Scotts' of Greenock, yard no. 509, for China Navigation Co. 29/03/1933: She was boarded by pirates off Newchang Bar, Manchuria; four officers were abducted and imprisoned in a junk, later third engineer officer was released with ransom demand. Five and half months later negotiations by Japanese and British succeeded in releasing the prisoners. 01/05/1950: Arrived at Hong Kong for scrapping. (A. Duncan, *Ships in Focus*)

1Sc-T3Cyl **NIGERIAN**
18/08/1925: Barclay Curle & Co., Glasgow, yard no. 612, for African & Eastern Trade Corp., London. 1935: Renamed *Kyrenia*. 1937: Renamed *Toronto City*. 01/07/1941: Serving on Admiralty service on meteorological duties when torpedoed and sunk in North Atlantic by *U-108* with loss of all crew. (Roy Fenton)

2Sc-MV **NORSEA**

09/09/1986: Govan Shipbuilders, yard no. 265, for North Sea Ferries for Hull–Rotterdam route. Largest and last passenger vessel built in UK since *QE2*. Sister *Norsun* launched by Nippon Kokan at Yokohama, carried 800 Nissan cars on delivery voyage to the Humber. P&O finally bought all shares in North Sea Ferries. *Norsea* renamed *Pride of York*, sister *Pride of Bruges*. (Author)

1Sc-ST **NOWSHERA (III)**

18/09/1954: Scotts' of Greenock, yard no. 665, for BI. With sister *Nyanza*, was large high-speed ship for UK–Australia trade: 18.01 knots on trials; *Nyanza* did 21.05 knots. 12/11/1963: Sank at Genoa when ship's side valve was left open. 17/04/1972: Transferred to P&O. 04/01/1974: To Arya National Shipping Lines, renamed *Arya Chehr*. 14/01/1976: Arrived at Shanghai for scrapping. (A. Duncan, *Ships in Focus*)

1Sc-ST **PANDO STRAIT**
11/06/1952: John Brown, Clydebank, yard no. 672, for P&O as *Sunda* (III). 26/10/1968: Renamed *Pando Strait*. 01/10/1971: Transferred to P&O General Cargo Division. 1972: Sold to Thos. W. Ward for demolition. 14/08/1972: Breaking up started at Inverkeithing. (A. Duncan, *Ships in Focus*)

1Sc-ST **PHEMIUS (II)**
06/09/1921: Scotts' of Greenock, yard no. 504, for Alfred Holt. 11/1932: Drifted for five days in hurricane in Caribbean, lost her funnel and was severely battered, Scotts'-built tanker *Narragansett* (yard no. 376, 1903) poured oil on seas. 12/11/1932: Reached Kingston. 19/12/1943: Torpedoed by *U-515* south of Accra; 5 crew and 18 passengers killed. (A. Duncan, *Ships in Focus*)

1Sc-MV **PORT BURNIE**
17/08/1965: Barclay Curle & Co., Whiteinch, yard no. 2015, for Port Line Ltd. 10/03/1967: To Blue Star Port Lines (Management). Port Line being part of Cunard, passed to Trafalgar House Investments Ltd in August 1971. 1972: To Afromar Inc., Piraeus, with *Port Albany* and *Port Huon*, renamed *Angeliki*. 1993: Renamed *Skopelus*. 02/08/1993: Arrived at Alang and scrapped. (A. Duncan, *Ships in Focus*)

2Sc-MV **PROMETHEUS (III)**
21/05/1925: Scotts' of Greenock, yard no. 525, for Alfred Holt. 26/02/1941: Attacked by German aircraft 270 miles from Rockall. 1957: To Janus Compania Naviera S.A., Panama, renamed *Janus*, but laid up at Alicante short time later. 10/1958: Caught fire, towed out of harbour and extinguished. 1959: Sold for demolition at Genoa. (A. Duncan, *Ships in Focus*)

4Sc-ST **QUEEN ELIZABETH**
27/09/1938: John Brown, Clydebank, yard no. 552, for Cunard White Star Steamship Co.'s North Atlantic service. As trooper carried 811,324 passengers and steamed 492,635 miles during war service between April 1941 and March 1946, often with around 15,000 aboard. 16/10/1946: Re-entered service. 1970: To Seawise Foundations Ltd, Nassau (C.Y. Tung). 09/01/1972: Destroyed by fire at Hong Kong harbour. (Author)

2Sc-T3Cyl **RAJULA**
22/09/1926: Barclay Curle & Co., Glasgow, yard no. 614, for BI; initially for Madras–Singapore service. 03/1938: Requisitioned as personnel ship. 30/08/1974: Arrived at Bombay for scrapping. After 35 years she was refitted by Mitsubishi at Kobe; no BI ship gave longer service and carried more passengers in peace and war. 30/08/1974: Arrived at Bombay for scrapping. (James Souter)

2-ScMV **RANGITANE (II)**

30/06/1949: John Brown, Clydebank, yard no. 648, for New Zealand Shipping Co. 22/05/1968: Sold to Astroguarda Cia. Nav. S.A., Piraeus; renamed *Jan*. 08/1968: To Taiwanese breakers. 09/1968: Re-sold and renamed *Oriental Esmeralda*. January to April 1969: Refitted at Hong Kong and entered round-the-world service from San Diego. 10/02/1976: Laid up at Hong Kong. 02/04/1976: Arrived at Kaohsiung for scrapping, which was started on 21 June 1976. (A. Duncan, *Ships in Focus*)

2Sc-Q4Cyl **RAWALPINDI**
26/03/1925: Harland and Wolff, Greenock, yard no. 660, for P&O. 26/08/1939: Requisitioned as AMC, converted at Royal Albert Dock, London. After funnel removed and eight 6in and two 3in guns fitted. 23/11/1939: Ran into German battlecruisers *Gneisenau* and *Scharnhorst* SE of Iceland and after 40 minutes was sunk by *Scharnhorst*. 40 officers and 226 ratings lost. (A. Duncan, *Ships in Focus*)

1Sc-MV **SANG FAJAR**
23/04/1947: A. & J. Inglis, Pointhouse, Glasgow, yard no. 1353, as *Soochow* for China Navigation Co. Designed for trade around China. This was terminated after the communist takeover, and in 1967 was sold to Pacific International, renamed *Kota Ratu*. Owned by Malaysian Shipping Corp. in 1975 and renamed *Sang Fajar*, her open sides aft were plated in, probably for additional passenger accommodation. 1984: Scrapped at Kaohsiung. (Author's collection)

1Sc-MV **SANGARA (III)**
07/03/1939: Scotts' of Greenock, yard no. 574, for Elder Dempster. 30/05/1940: Torpedoed by *U-60* whilst anchored at Accra, and settled on bottom. Salvaged and gutted by locals. Italian submarine *Enrico Tazzoli* fired at wreck but missed. Taken to Lagos, then Duala. 1945: Bought back by Elder Dempster. 04/1947: Back into service after rebuilding. 09/1960: Sold for scrapping at Preston. (A. Duncan, *Ships in Focus*)

1Sc-ST **SHENGKING (II)**
28/10/1931: Scotts' of Greenock, yard no. 554, for China Navigation Co. Designed for Tientsin service with strengthened ice-breaking bow. 07/1932: Aground in typhoon on Chimeng Island. Requisitioned during WWII and served mainly in Indian Ocean. In peacetime on Hong Kong–Shanghai and Hong Kong–Keelung routes. 1955: To Shun Cheong S.N. Co., renamed *Tai Po Shek*. 29/01/1958: Laid up in Hong Kong, scrapped the following year. (Author's collection)

1Sc-MV **SINGA SAILOR**
03/07/1970: Upper Clyde Shipbuilders, yard no. 844, as *Fresno City* for William Reardon Smith & Sons. 1982: Renamed *Olmeca*. 1988: Renamed *Singa Sailor* by Singa Swan Shipping Corp., Monrovia. 28/06/1994: For scrapping in China. (Chris Howell)

1Sc-MV **TAIYUAN (III)**
12/05/1949: Scotts' of Greenock, yard no. 646, for China Navigation Co. for their Australian service. Sister to *Changsha* (IV). Transferred to Sydney–Fiji route in 1970. Also 1970: Sold to Pacific International Lines Pte, Singapore, and renamed *Kota Sahabat*. Converted to a sheep carrier in 1978. 10/03/1980: Delivered to Kaohsiung for scrapping. (A. Duncan, *Ships in Focus*)

2Sc-ST **UGANDA (II)**
15/01/1952: Barclay Curle & Co., Glasgow, yard no. 720, for BI's UK–East Africa service. 1967–68: Converted to educational cruise ship at Hamburg. 13/04/1982: Charted by Admiralty as hospital ship in Falklands War. Back cruising in September, then chartered as link between Falklands and Ascension. 29/04/1986: To Triton Shipping Co., Barbados, renamed *Triton*. 22/08/1986: Driven ashore in typhoon near Kaohsiung and capsized, then scrapped. (A. Duncan, *Ships in Focus*)

2Sc-ST **UMGAZI**
30/11/1939: Greenock Dockyard, yard no. 437. 30/03/1940: Registered to Scottish Shire Line Ltd as *Lanarkshire*. 01/03/1959: Transferred to Bullard, King & Co. Ltd, renamed *Umgazi*. 12/1950: To Springbok Line Ltd. 01/1960: To Springbok Shipping Co. Ltd, Cape Town, renamed *Grysbok*. 01/07/1961: Managed by S.A. Marine Corp., renamed *South African Farmer*. 20/01/1963: Arrived Aioi, Japan, for scrapping. (J.G. Callis)

2Sc-STE **VICEROY OF INDIA**
15/09/1928: Alexander Stephen & Sons Ltd, Glasgow, yard no. 519, for P&O. Name was proposed to be *Taj Mahal.* Designed for Bombay service but also for cruising. 12/11/1940: Requisitioned as troopship and converted on the Clyde. 11/11/1942: Torpedoed and sunk by *U-407* off Oran; two officers and two firemen lost with remainder picked up by HMS *Boadicea*. (A. Duncan, *Ships in Focus*)

1Sc-ST **WARWICKSHIRE (II)**
14/08/1947: Fairfield, Glasgow. 14/07/1965: As yard no. 733 for Bibby Line, reverted to steam single screw after preferring diesel propulsion for over 27 years. 1965: To Aegean SS Co., Typados Bros, Piraeus, and converted to car ferry, renamed *Hania* but listed as *Chanea*. 1966: Owners bankrupt, laid up at Perama, derelict and later scrapped. (A. Duncan, *Ships in Focus*)

2Sc-T3cyl **WOODARRA (I)**
12/07/1919: Barclay Curle & Co., Glasgow, yard no. 572, as G-type standard refrigerated ship originally to be named *War Apollo*. Had accommodation for 39 cadets. 21/08/1929: To Blue Star for £60,000, renamed *Fresno Star*. 07/1947: After many grounding and mishaps but incident-free war service from June 1940 to March 1946, she arrived at Inverkeithing for scrapping. (A. Duncan, *Ships in Focus*)

1Sc-MV **YAQUI**
24/03/1970: Upper Clyde Shipbuilders, Govan, yard no. 841, as *Prince Rupert* for Reardon Smith Line, Cardiff. Other names: *Yaqui* (1982); *Singa Sky* (1982); *Zhong Nong Xin* (2004); *Herun* (2005). (Chris Howell)

1Sc-MV **TREVALGAN (IV)**
06/12/1960: William Hamilton & Co., Port Glasgow, yard no. 523, for Hain Steamship Co. Ltd. Later registered under Hain-Nourse Ltd with P&O Steamship Cargo Division as managers, then registered under Peninsular & Oriental Steam Navigation Co. 05/01/1973: To Evalend Shipping Co. S.A., Greece, renamed *Lendoudis Evangelos*. 1985: To Bangladeshi breakers. 07/03/1985: Scrapped at Bhatiary. (Malcolm Cranfield)

2

Tankers

The Clyde's versatility saw oil tankers produced from all the yards, big and small, but it has to be said that there appeared to be an assumption that the post-war tanker building boom would soon disappear. Ironically, in the boom era following the closure of the Suez Canal in 1956, a record tonnage of 377,120grt was being built abroad for UK owners. Space restrictions due to the multiplicity of laterally sited berths and limited space on the landward side, often due to boundaries and public roads, inhibited the construction of the largest sizes. One answer was offered by Lithgows when they organised the layout of their yard for the construction of the ship in two halves, which, after being launched, was then joined up afloat.

1Sc-T3Cyl **ALCHYMIST (II)**
30/11/1934: A. & J. Inglis, Pointhouse, Glasgow, yard no. 1288, as *Empire Orkney* for MOWT, managed by C. Rowbotham & Sons. 10/1949: Acquired by F.T. Everard & Sons Ltd and renamed *Alchymist*. 03/05/1959: Arrived at Brugse Scheepssloperij for scrapping. (Trevor Jones, Malcolm Cranfield)

1Sc-MV **ALIGNITY**

12/06/1945: A. & J. Inglis, Pointhouse, Glasgow, yard no. 1301, as *Empire Fitzroy* for MOWT, managed by Anglo-Saxon Petroleum Co. Ltd. 1946: Managed by British Tanker Co. Ltd. 12/1946: Managed by Anglo-Saxon Petroleum Co. Ltd. 1949: Managed by Coastal Tanker, London. 09/1952: Sold to F.T. Everard & Sons, renamed *Alignity*. 11/1971: Sold to Hughes Bolckow for scrapping at Blyth, arriving 10 November 1971. (Malcolm Cranfield)

1Sc-MV **ANONITY**

30/04/1945: A. & J. Inglis, Pointhouse, Glasgow, yard no. 1300, as tanker *Empire Campden* for MOWT, for Far East service. 05/1947: To F.T. Everard & Sons Ltd and renamed *Anonity*. 06/1966: To S.J. & J.S. Latsis, Piraeus, renamed *Petrola II*. 1969: To Chryssochoides & M. Chalkiopoulos, Piraeus, renamed *Kalymnos*. 12/04/1970: Wrecked on east coast of Rhodes, salvaged and towed to Piraeus. 27/05/1970: Sold for scrapping at Salmina. (Author)

1Sc-MV **BORDER SHEPHERD**
31/03/1960: Lithgows Ltd, Port Glasgow, yard no. 1130, for Lowland Tanker Co. Ltd. First BP tanker with bridge and accommodation aft. 1978: Sold to BP Tanker Co. Ltd. 1981: To Alzimar Shipping Co. S.A., renamed *Mariverda IV*. 1883: transferred to Pyramid Navigation Co. E.S.A., Egypt, renamed *Al Nabila II*. 26/05/1993: At Alang for scrapping. (Malcolm Cranfield)

1Sc-MV **BRITISH INTEGRITY (I)**
22/06/1937: Harland and Wolff, Govan, yard no. 972G, for British Tanker Co. 1957: Renamed *Gaelic Integrity* and managed by J.J. Denholm, Glasgow. 24/05/1958: Arrived at Hendrik-Ido-Ambacht, Holland, for scrapping. (World Ship Society Photo Library (WSSPL))

1Sc-ST **BRITISH MARINER**
23/04/1963: John Brown, Clydebank, yard no. 715, for British Tanker Co. 09/11/1975: Arrived at Kaohsiung for scrapping. (Author)

1Sc-MV **BRITISH ROBIN (I)**
19/11/1959: Lithgows Ltd, Port Glasgow, yard no. 1126, for BP Tanker Co. Ltd. One of 14 similar 15,500dwt tankers. 03/1960: Transferred to Clyde Charter Co. Ltd. 1972: Transferred back to BP. 1977: Sold to Locofrance Service S.A., renamed *Lot*. 1983: Sold to Fal Bunkering Co. Ltd, Dubai, renamed *Fal XI*. 08/07/1986: Drove ashore at Clifton Beach, Pakistan, whilst awaiting scrapping. (Malcolm Cranfield)

1Sc-MV **BRITISH SWIFT**
24/06/1959: Scotts' of Greenock, yard no. 681, for Clyde Charter Co. Ltd. 1972: Transferred to BP Tanker Co. Ltd. 1973: Sold to Erynflex Ltd. 1977: To Noah Shipping Co., Iran. 2005: renamed *Noah VI*. Relegated to a static role and used in Iranian film *Iron Island*. (Author)

1Sc-MV **NEREIDE**
22/12/1953: Scotts' of Greenock, yard no. 661, as *Border Hunter* for Lowland Tanker Co. Ltd; cost £827,070. First ship in the new group was Scotts'-built *Border Regiment* of an initial batch of 10 tankers for BP charter. 06/04/1970: To Nereide Shipping Corp., renamed *Nereide*. 1975: To Alfonso Garcia, Spain, for demolition. 11/04/1975: Arrived at Bilbao for scrapping. (Malcolm Cranfield)

1Sc-ST **QUEDA**
14/08/1958: Scotts' of Greenock, yard no. 677, as product tanker for BI, although nominal owners were the New Zealand Shipping Co. Ltd. 09/05/1963: Managed by Trident Tankers Ltd. 14/07/1969: To Clyde Shipping Co., Monrovia, renamed *Saint Michel*. 1971: To Petroleos de Peru, renamed *9 de Octobre*. 1974: Converted to liquid petroleum gas tanker. 05/1981: Dismantled prior to scrapping at Calloa. (A. Duncan, *Ships in Focus*)

1Sc-ST **SHELL NAIGUATA**
12/05/1960: Fairfield, Govan, yard no. 785, for Shell de Venezuela; sister ship *Shell Aramare*, yard no. 784. Designed to supply crude oil to Curacao and the new refinery at Punta Cardon, Venezuela, observing Venezuelan requirements to have call sign painted on bows below ship's name. 1976: Sold and renamed *Naiguata*. 31/05/1979: Arrived at Kaohsiung for scrapping. (Author)

3

Naval and Auxiliary

The River Clyde had a long association of building for the Admiralty; Scotts', in fact, can possibly be credited with the Clyde's first steam frigate for the Royal Navy – HMS *Greenock*, launched in 1849 – although in 1838–39 they had built the machinery for HMS *Hecla* and *Hecate*, built in the naval dockyards.

Nearly without exception all the shipyards on the Clyde built naval vessels, ranging from the largest capital ships to a wide variety of other types, almost exclusively during the Second World War. Naturally, the majority of capital ships, such as battleships, battlecruisers and aircraft carriers, were built by the larger concerns, but we should not forget the part played by the smaller yards in the construction of the varied and ever more sophisticated assortment of smaller and vital front-line and support vessels.

2Sc-MV + Elec Motors **HMS ARTFUL P456**
22/05/1947: Scotts' of Greenock, yard no. 623. Only one of class completed without any gun armament. Designed primarily for Far East service with improved habitability and endurance; fabricated in all-welded sections. Operating depth of 500ft, but able to reach 600ft. Only two were completed prior to end of WWII. 23/06/1972: Sold for breaking up at Queenborough. (WSSPL)

1Sc-T4Cyl **HMS ARABIS (II) K385**
28/10/1943: George Brown & Co., Greenock, yard no. 227. Modified Flower class corvette. Building time was 12 months 18 days and the ship was completed on 16 March 1944. Transferred to New Zealand Navy on completion as HMNZS *Arabis*. 1948: Decommissioned. 1951: Scrapped at Grays. (D. Brown)

4Sc-ST **HMAS AUSTRALIA**
17/03/1927: John Brown, Clydebank, yard no. 512. Sister to Kent class cruiser. Their structural strength also allowed them to maintain 34 knots in most weathers. 21/10/1944: Badly damaged by a kamikaze and out of action until January 1945. More kamikaze damage in same month, with heavy casualties; repairs at Sydney and UK. 1955: Towed from Sydney and scrapped at Barrow. (Author's collection)

1Sc-3Tycl **HMS BARDSEY T273**
17/07/1943: Fleming & Ferguson, Paisley, yard no. 601. Isles class anti-submarine minesweeping trawler. 1946: Disarmed and converted to a wreck dispersal vessel. 1950: Converted to a tank-cleaning vessel based at Malta as seen here. 03/1959: Sold to Baileys of Malta for commercial use. 1971: Scrapped. (WSSPL)

1Sc-T4Cyl **HMS BLUEBELL K80**
24/04/1939: Fleming & Ferguson, Paisley, yard no. 559. Flower class corvette. Served as escort on no less than 11 Russian convoys. 13/02/1945: In Convoy JW64 towed the torpedoed HMS *Denbigh Castle* to Kola Inlet. 17/02/1945: As escort in Convoy RA64 torpedoed by *U-711* off Kola Inlet, blew up and sank with only one survivor, 90 lost. (WSSPL)

2Sc-ST **HMS CAVENDISH D15**
12/04/1944: John Brown, Clydebank, yard no. 606. 'C' class destroyer. Ex-HMS *Sybil*. 1963: First ship fitted with Seacat GWS replacing the 40mm gun mounting. 01/1994: Full modernisation commenced: Mark VI installed on new bridge structure, two three-barrelled Squid in place of X gun aft. Fishery protection for a period off Iceland. 07/08/67: Arrived at Blyth for scrapping by Hughes Bolckow. (WSSPL)

2Sc-ST **HMS COLUSSUS**
09/04/1910: Scotts' of Greenock, yard no. 430, as a Colossus class battleship. The first dreadnought to be built on the Clyde. The position of the funnel caused smoke nuisance to the gunnery control position, and in 1912 was heightened. 31/05/1916: Received two hits at Jutland. From 1919 was a cadet training ship. 06/10/1928: To Ward at Briton Ferry for scrapping. (WSSPL)

2Sc-ST **HMS DIAMOND D35**
14/06/1950: John Brown, Clydebank, yard no. 632. Daring class destroyer. Builder's first all-welded ship; 220-volt AC electrics. Noise trials required docking five times, with special glass ports, changing propellers and instruments fitted to investigate. 29/09/1953: Damaged bow in collision with HMS *Swiftsure* off Iceland. 05/1963: Turbines sabotaged at Chatham. 12/1969: Paid off. 09/11/1981: Towed to Medway for scrapping. (Author)

1Sc-MV **EMPIRE MACRAE**
21/06/1943: Lithgows Ltd, Port Glasgow, yard no. 992. 09/1943: Completed as a merchant aircraft carrier (MAC); Hain Line managers. 27/01/1947: To Moller Line London. 21/05/1947: To Alpha South Africa Steamship Co. Ltd. 30/06/1947: Renamed *Alpha Zambesi*. 15/11/1949: To Motor Lines Clunies Shipping Co., Greenock. Had following names: *Tobon* and *Despina P.* 02/05/1978: Arrived for breaking up at Kaohsiung. (Roy Fenton)

2Sc-ST **HMS GLASGOW**
20/06/1936: Scotts' of Greenock, yard no. 564. Town class cruiser. 03/12/1940: Hit by two aerial torpedoes at Suda Bay; repairs at Alexandria, Singapore and USA. 30/03/1943: Captured blockade runner *Regensburg*. 12/1943: With HMS *Enterprise* sank three German destroyers in Bay of Biscay. 25/06/1944: Damaged by shore batteries off Normandy. 1956: Paid off. 05/07/1958: Arrived at Blyth for scrapping. (WSSPL)

2Sc-ST **HMS LION C34**
02/09/1944: Scotts' of Greenock, yard no. 611, as HMS *Defence*, a Tiger class cruiser. Laid up 1946–54 after launch and completed by Swan Hunter in 1960 at a cost of £1,375,000 (original building cost £1,476,898) as modernised cruiser HMS *Lion C20*. Conversion to helicopter cruiser considered but abandoned and put on disposal list in 1975. 24/04/1975: Arrived at Inverkeithing for scrapping. (Author)

1Sc-MV **BAMORA (II)**
06/09/1960: Harland and Wolff, Govan, Glasgow; yard no. 1612G for BI. One of five distinctive sisters for Australia–India and Persian Gulf trades. 1971: To Indo-Pacific Corp., Liberia, renamed *Sumatra Breeze*, then *Trikora Djaya*. 1973: To South East Asia Shipping (Pte) Ltd, renamed *Mahabakti*. 1980: To Lyttleton Shipping Corp., renamed *Dina*. 1982: To China Yangtze Shipping Co. renamed *Yang Zi Jiang No. 3*, in service 2007. (Chris Howell)

1Sc-ST **BENLAWERS (IV)**
27/03/1944: Charles Connell & Co. as yard no. 444, Glasgow, for Ben Line Steamers. 06/1944: Completed and handed over. 20/02/1968: Sold and arrived at Kaohsiung, Taiwan, for scrapping by Nan Seng Steel Enterprise, after a credible 24 years' service as a turbine steamer. (Painting by the author)

1Sc-MV **BENSTAC**

20/11/1967: Charles Connell & Co., Glasgow, yard no. 512, for Ben Line Steamers. This Bendearg class had engines and bridge three-quarters aft and could also carry containers on deck. 09/1982: Sold to Papanaves Shipping Co. (Hellas), Piraeus, Greece, and renamed *John P.* 13/04/1985: 250 miles east of Brazil had explosion in engine room and sank en route from Buenos Aires to Lobito. (Chris Howell)

1Sc-MV **GEESTCAPE**

27/05/1975: Scotstoun Marine yard no. 206 for Charles Connell & Co., Denholm Ship Management Ltd, as *Loch Maree*. Had around a dozen owners or managers from new and bore following names: 1981: *Al-Salamia*; 1984: *Langelle*; 1986: *Geestcape*; 1993: *Eastcape*; 1996: *Pacific Gala*; 1996: *Rio Negro Valley*; 2001: *Ice Music*. 13/10/2006: Arrived at Chittagong for scrapping. (Malcolm Cranfield)

2Sc-ST **TOLMI**
18/03/1949: Lithgows Ltd, Port Glasgow, yard no. 1029, as *Biographer* for T. & J. Harrison. 17/09/1964: To Tolmi Compania Naviera S.A. Panama, renamed *Tolmi*. Had a long history of machinery breakdowns since sold. 12/05/1970: Aground Bangara River, India, and refloated. 12/1973: Broke down in South China Sea, towed to Singapore by *Salviper*, beyond repair and sold. 12/01/1974: Arrived at Kaohsiung for scrapping. (Malcolm Cranfield)

1Sc-MV **FORT ROSALIE A385**
9/12/1976: Scotts' of Greenock, yard no. 737, as *Fort Grange* an AFES type (ammunition, food, explosives including nuclear) Fleet Replenishment Ship, Ice Class 3, with at least six Replenishment at Sea (RAS) points. 2000: Renamed *Fort Rosalie* to avoid confusion with *Fort George*. (Terry Egleton)

1Sc-DEMV **RMAS NEWTON A367**
25/06/1975: Scotts' of Greenock for oceanographic trials and research. Could lay cables and had cable tanks with winches and bow rollers for deployment. Fitted with nozzle rudder and retractable bow thruster. Later had modifications to suit training of amphibious forces. From 1996 was operated by Serco Denholm as SD *Newton*. 18/08/2012: Towed by Dutch tug *Pearl* to Ghent for scrapping. (Daniel Ferro)

2Sc-VS **JUPITER (III)**
27/11/1973: James Lamont & Co., Port Glasgow, yard no. 418, for Caledonian MacBrayne. Second in fleet to have this type of propulsion, *Keppel* being the first. For Gourock–Dunoon service, later Wemyss Bay–Rothesay service, also relief vessel to Arran. The flying bridge was added in 1974 to give better visibility aft when berthing. 2011: Towed to Grenaa in Denmark for scrapping. (Graham Wilson)

2Sc-MV **LOCH SHIRA**
08/12/2006: Ferguson Shipbuilders, Port Glasgow, yard no. 721, for Caledonian MacBrayne. Car/passenger ferry used on the Largs–Cumbrae service with capacity for 250 passengers and rated maximum of 36 cars, the slipway at Largs being modified to accommodate her. Manoeuvrability is ensured with two Voith Schneider propellers. She represented a total investment of £6.4 million. (Author)

PS **WAVERLEY**
02/10/1946: A. & J. Inglis, Pointhouse, Glasgow, yard no. 1330P, for the LNER as a Clyde excursion steamer. Latter services on the Clyde in 1974 were under Caledonian MacBrayne flag. 1973: Laid up then sold for £1 to Waverley Steam Navigation Co., re-entering service on 22/05/1975. Operated by Waverley Excursions Ltd since 1980 as the last seagoing paddler in the world. (Author)

1Sc-MV **ATLANTIS INS109**
1973: Completed by the Campbeltown Shipyard at Trench Point, Campbeltown, as *Cavalier* INS109. 1981: Renamed *Ardent* INS109. 1986: Renamed *Atlantis* INS109. 2002: Decommissioned. This yard was on the site of the earlier Campbeltown Shipbuilding Co. established in 1877 which built 116 ships until closure in 1922, the largest being the 4,363-ton *Roquelle* in 1918. (Author)

2Sc-MV **DALMARNOCK (II)**
14/09/1970: James Lamont & Co., Port Glasgow, yard no. 412, as sludge carrier for Glasgow Corporation. Regulations effective from 1 January 1999 banned disposal at sea and she was sold to Northumbrian Water Board, renamed *Bran Sands*. 2007: Sold to Mettle Energy & Gas (Ryan Ship Management Ltd), Lagos, and converted to bunkering tanker, renamed *Efeomo* in 2008. (Author)

2Sc-MV **GARROCH HEAD**
17/03/1977: James Lamont & Co., Port Glasgow, yard no. 431, for Glasgow Corporation to carry sludge downriver for dumping; following tradition, she could carry deck passengers to enjoy the Clyde scenery. This practice, which had gone on since 1904 without problem, was later banned. Sold in 1999 to Unibros Shipping Corp., believed now in service as water carrier in Africa. (Author)

2Sc-DEMV **PACNORSE I**
07/04/1979: Scotts' of Greenock, yard no. 746, for Pacnorse Drilling Bermuda Corp. Dynamically positioned drill ship. Had numerous owners and managers since new. 1966: Sold to Falcon Drilling Corp. Inc., Houston, renamed *Peregrine II*. 2002: Sold to Frontier Drilling ASA, Bahamas; three years later to Frontier Drilling ASA. Renamed *Frontier Deepwater* and now *Noble Phoenix*. (Author)

1Sc-DEMV **SCOTIA (IV)**
1998: Ferguson Shipbuilders, Port Glasgow, yard no. 704, for Scottish Fishery Research vessel, named by the Queen Mother at Aberdeen for Marine Scotland for operations in North Sea and NE Atlantic. Fitted with a wide array of equipment for fish sampling and evaluation of stocks. (Author)

TRITSCH TRATSCH
1971: James McGruer Cylinder, Dunbartonshire. Designed by the noted yacht builder as a fast, comfortable six-berth, 41ft overall sloop for Dr Otto Glaser of Ireland. 1972: Sold to a Scottish yachtsman for use in Scotland and France. 1974: To US owner and after refit at Falmouth was taken across to Maine. Renamed *Bartholomew*. (Author)

2Sc-CoDoG **KD HANG JEBAT F24**
18/12/1967: Yarrow Shipbuilders Ltd, Scotstoun, yard no. 2325. For Royal Malaysian Navy. CODAG machinery installed. First of two general purpose frigates built to their own design. Built taking advantage of advances in miniaturised electronics and propulsion to save manning costs. The A/S Limbo mortar well aft can be covered over to take a helicopter. Renamed KD *Rahmat*; now a museum ship. (Author)

2Sc-ST **HMS JAVELIN G61**
21/12/1938: John Brown, Clydebank, yard no. 557; name intended to be *Kashmir*. Involved in Dunkirk evacuation; hit by two torpedoes in English Channel which reduced her length to 155ft; rebuilt at Devonport. Involved in numerous actions in Mediterranean, Indian Ocean, Palestine blockade etc. 21/02/1948: Used for shock trials in Scottish lochs and later to BISCO for scrapping. 11/1949: Started scrapping at Troon. (WSSPL)

2Sc-MV **MERMAID**
29/12/1966: Yarrow Shipbuilders Ltd, Scotstoun, yard no. 2284. Launched without ceremony in 1966 as *Black Star*; originally built for Ghana for ex-President Nkrumah as flagship and yacht, but was deposed before launch, completed and laid up. 04/1972: Bought by RN from Yarrows and refitted at Chatham. 04/1977: To Malaysian Navy, renamed KD *Hang Tuah*. (Author)

1ScT34cyl **HMS OAKHAM CASTLE F530**
20/07/1944: A. & J. Inglis, Pointhouse, Glasgow, yard no. 1236. Castle class corvette. 08/1957: One of four Castle class vessels, replacing the Flower class corvettes, as Atlantic Ocean weather ship *Weather Reporter* based at Greenock. 1977: Sold to Tees Marine for scrapping in Middlesbrough. (WSSPL)

2Sc-MV+Elec. Motors **HMAS OTWAY (II)**
29/11/1966: Scotts' of Greenock, yard no. 699, an Oberon class submarine for Royal Australian Navy, the second of six built for them by Scotts'. On delivery voyage was first RAN submarine to round Cape of Good Hope. 17/02/1994: Paid off and sold in November; upper half shell was moved in sections and joined and dedicated at Holbrook to serve as a memorial. (Chris Howell)

4Sc-ST **HMS RAMILLIES**
12/09/1916: William Beardmore & Co., Dalmuir, yard no. 516. Royal Sovereign class battleship with large bulges extending almost up to battery. Damaged during launching. Towed to Liverpool for completion by Cammell Laird. 30/05/1942: Torpedoed by Japanese midget submarine in Diego Suarez Bay; repairs at Durban took 12 months. Took part in D-Day bombardment. 20/03/1948: Sold for scrapping at Cairn Ryan and Troon. (Author's collection)

4Sc-ST **HMS REPULSE**
08/01/1916: John Brown, Clydebank, yard no. 443. 10/12/1941: At sea without adequate air cover she was sunk by Japanese torpedo bombers off Malaya. Order was initially placed with Palmers, but without a slip long enough the order was transferred to Browns. Built in 18 months since laid down. 15/09/1916: On trials where she achieved a speed of 31.73 knots. (WSSPL)

1Sc-ST **RESOURCE A480**
11/02/1966: Scotts' of Greenock, yard no. 697. Fleet replenishment ship for Royal Fleet Auxiliary, sister to RFA *Regent*. In the Falkland Islands conflict, stored munitions including WE.177A live nuclear weapons. First front-line RFAs to carry a permanent helicopter. 1997: To Harlequin Shipping Ltd. 24/06/1997: Left Devonport, renamed *Resourceful*, for voyage to breakers. 20/08/1997: Arrived for scrapping by R.K. Industries at Alang. (Author)

1Sc-T3Cyl **ROWANOL**
15/05/1946: Lobnitz & Co., Renfrew, yard no. 1091; laid down as *Ebonol* (II) for Admiralty. Ol class tanker. 10/12/1971: Arrived at Bruges for scrapping. (Author)

2Sc-ST **KNMS SVENNER GO3**
01/06/1943: Scotts' of Greenock, yard no. 601; launched as HMS *Shark* but handed over to Norwegian Navy in 1944 and renamed. 06/06/1944: Torpedoed and sunk off Normandy on D-Day by German torpedo boats *T28*, *Mowe* and *Jaguar*; she broke in two and sank quickly. Her anchor has been recovered and forms a memorial at Sword beach. (WSSPL)

4Sc-ST **HMS TIGER**
15/12/1913: John Brown, Clydebank, yard no. 418. Exceeded her estimated cost of £2,593,095. Originally to be a Lion class battlecruiser. To expedite completion continuous night and weekend working introduced. Last RN coal-burning capital ship. Until HMS *Hood* was launched in 1918 she was largest ship in RN. 1932: Scrapped at Inverkeithing. (WSSPL)

4

Coastal Cargo, Passenger Ships and Ferries

The grouping together of passenger-carrying vessels, ferries and cargo carriers has been adopted for the same reasons given in the first chapter. As such, this chapter will inevitably cover a wide range of types.

The builders and operators on the River Clyde were responsible for the development of the coastal passenger and excursion vessel to its highest degree of attainment, as exemplified by the many handsome and popular paddle and screw steamers, a legacy which still has resonance today, in memory at least.

2-Sc-MV **ABERCRAIG**
1939: Fleming & Ferguson, Paisley, yard no. 550, as passenger and car ferry for River Tay, running between Newport on Tay and Dundee. Redundant after opening of the Tay Road Bridge in August 1966. Following the opening of the Tay Road Bridge she was sold to Malta and used as a ferry. (Author)

1Sc-MV **ACTIVITY (I)**

16/09/1931: George Brown & Co., Greenock, yard no. 181, for F.T. Everard & Sons. 1962: Re-engined. 02/1966: Sold to M. Gigilinis & D. Kalkasinas and renamed *Giankaros*. 1971: Sold to J. Calafatis and renamed *Ioannis K.* 1977: Sold to P. Panagopoulos. She was deleted from the register in 1992. (A. Duncan, *Ships in Focus*)

1Sc-T3cyl **AMPANG**

1925: George Brown & Co., Greenock, yard no. 146. Same owners and subsequent re-assembly as *Rengang* but fitted with a triple-expansion reciprocating steam engine. 11/02/1942: Left Singapore for Batavia, but out of fuel called at Palembang; after attack on city by Japanese she was abandoned on 14 February 1942. Crew crossed overland through Sumatra to Osthaven then across Sunda Strait to Batavia. (D. Brown)

1Sc-MV **ANTRIM COAST**

17/12/1936: Ardrossan Dockyard, yard no. 364, for Coast Lines, serving Liverpool–London via Belfast and Cork. Renamed *Sark Coast* and later *Miltiadis*. 15/01/1973: Scrapped. (B. Fielden, J. & M. Clarkson)

2Sc-MV **BUTE (VI)**
28/09/1954: Ailsa Shipbuilding Co., yard no. 481, for Caledonian Steam Packet Co. One of ABC car ferries on the Gourock–Dunoon route. 1959: After hold plated over to give additional vehicle capacity. 1973: To Caledonian MacBrayne Holdings Ltd. 1975–77: Serviced the MacAlpine construction yard at Ardyne. 1980: Sold to Gerasimos Phetouris, Greece, renamed *Mediterranean Sun*. 01/1981: Damaged and scrapped. (Author)

PS **CALEDONIA (II)**
01/02/1934: William Denny & Bros, Dumbarton, yard no. 1266, for Caledonia Steam Packet Co. 12/1939: Requisitioned as minesweeper, renamed HMS *Goatfell*, and then as AA flak ship. 05/1945: Back to owners for 12-month refit. 11/02/1970: Sold to Arnott & Young for scrapping at Dalmuir. 11/1971: Converted to restaurant ship on Thames by Bass Charrington brewery. 07/1980: Scrapped at Sittingbourne after burned out. (Author)

1Sc-2Cyl **CLAYMORE (I)**
14/07/1881: J. & G. Thomson, Clydebank, yard no. 185, for David MacBrayne. A noted beauty and a great favourite serving the west Highlands. She was initially on Glasgow–Stornaway route via Greenock, Oban and other various mainland ports. Withdrawn in 1930; plans to convert to a hotel in a Highland loch never materialised and was sold for £75 for scrapping at Bo'ness in 1931. (WSSPL)

1Sc-2Cyl **DAVAAR**
18/05/1885: London & Glasgow Engineering & Iron Shipbuilding Co., Govan, yard no. 247, for Campbeltown & Glasgow Steam Packet Stock Co. 1903: Re-boilered and original two funnels replaced by single funnel, improving her looks. Served Campbeltown from a number of ports on lower Clyde during WWI because of the anti-submarine boom. 1940: Taken for use as a blockship at Newhaven but finally scrapped in 1943. (Author's collection)

PS **DUCHESS OF FIFE (II)**
09/05/1903: Fairfield, Govan, yard no. 432, for Caledonian Steam Packet Co. for Gourock–Kyles route. First paddle steamer built by Fairfield, designed by their naval architect Percy Hillhouse. 1916: Requisitioned by Admiralty as minesweeper, returned in 1919. 1923: To London, Midland & Scottish Railway Co. 1939: To Caledonian Steam Packet Co. 1940: Requisitioned as minesweeper, returned 1945. 15/09/1953: For scrapping at Port Glasgow. (Author's collection)

PS **DUCHESS OF HAMILTON (I)**
10/04/1890: William Denny & Bros, Dumbarton, yard no. 439, for Caledonian Steam Packet Co. She initiated the trend of extending the promenade deck to the bow. She opened their Ardrossan–Arran route. A popular ship, when replaced she became a club and excursion steamer and later on the Arrochar run. Requisitioned for trooping in March 1915, later as minesweeper. 19/11/1915: Mined and sunk off Harwich. (Author's collection)

PS **DUCHESS OF MONTROSE (I)**
08/05/1902: John Brown, Clydebank, yard no. 352, for Caledonian Steam Packet Co. Originally intended for excursions from Ayr, but served on many routes. 02/1915: Requisitioned by Admiralty and used initially to carry troops to France; later converted to minesweeper with pennant number PP585. 18/03/1917: Struck a mine off Dunkirk and sank. (Author's collection)

3Sc-ST **DUCHESS OF MONTROSE (II)**
05/05/1932: Harland and Wolff, Govan, yard no. 920G, the only Clyde steamer built by the yard, for Caledonian Steam Packet Co. She made over 20 knots on trials and used mainly on excursions on the lower firth. A troop tender and on Stranraer–Larne route in WWII. 1946: Back into service. 1956: Converted to oil firing. 24/04/1974: Arrived at Troon for scrapping. (Author)

2Sc-MV **EIGG**
12/12/1974: James Lamont & Co., Port Glasgow, yard no. 423, for Caledonian MacBrayne and one of the very handy Island class ferries. Usually on Oban–Lismore sailing but initially took the Portree–Raasay service on withdrawal of the *Loch Arkaig* and followed the usual round of varied duties as required. Was re-engined and altered with a higher wheelhouse than in the photograph. (Author)

PS **SANDOWN**
01/05/1934: William Denny & Bros, Dumbarton, yard no. 1272, for Southern Railway Co., Portsmouth, for Portsmouth and Southsea–Ryde, Isle of Wight service. Requisitioned in 1939 and served as minesweeper but converted to AA ship in 1942. 1945: Returned to service. 1966: Put up for sale, still a coal burner. 17/02/1966: Arrived at Antwerp towed by *Temi III*. 16/07/1966: Scrapped. (Author's collection)

2Sc-MV **GLEN SANNOX (III)**
30/04/1957: Ailsa Shipbuilding Co., Troon, yard no. 496, for Caledonian Steam Packet Co. for the Arran–Fairlie–Ardrossan route. Later in 1970 with a new stern ramp she took on a number of varied roles. 1971: Re-engined with Wichmann diesels by Hall Russell. 09/08/1989: Left Clyde as *Knooz* for Piraeus. Since 2000 seen lying sunken 70km south of Jeddah as *Al Basmala I*. (Author)

3Sc-ST **GLEN SANNOX (II)**
24/02/1925: William Denny & Bros, yard no. 1170, for London, Midland & Scottish Railway. With direct drive turbines she was the last Clyde steamer to have an open promenade deck. After takeover by Caledonian Steam Packet Co. in 1936 she was put on the Campbeltown–Ardrossan route but requisitioned during WWII. 28/07/1954: Towed from Greenock to Ghent for scrapping. (Author's collection)

1Sc-Osc **IONA (III)**
10/05/1864: J. & G. Thomson, Govan, yard no. 77, for David Hutcheson & Co., Glasgow, on the Glasgow–Ardishaig mail route; at 255ft long was greater than any Clyde vessel of that era. 1875: Reconstructed by her builders. 1891: Re-boilered and fitted with lengthened and closer-spaced funnels. 1879: To David MacBrayne. 1936: Scrapped by Arnott & Young at Dalmuir. (Author's collection)

2Sc-MV **IONIC FERRY**
02/05/1958: William Denny & Bros, Dumbarton, yard no. 1493, for the Atlantic Steam Navigation Co.; with the earlier *Bardic Ferry*, she was the first of new type of drive-on vehicle ferries for the owner's Preston–Larne route. They loaded via a stern ramp and had space and crane on after deck for handling containers. Accommodation was provided for 55 passengers in two classes. (Author's collection)

1Sc-SS **KARATTA** (*Meeting of the Waters*)
25/07/1907: George Brown & Co., Greenock, yard no. 45, for Gulf SS Co., Adelaide. 1914: Coast Steamships Ltd, Port Adelaide. Designed for Port Adelaide–Kangaroo Island service and served for over 50 years. 08/11/1961: Last voyage. 03/12/1961: Sold to Heines Metals Ltd for scrapping. (D. Brown)

1Sc-MV **KOORAKA** (*White Gum*)
07/03/1925: George Brown & Co., Greenock, yard no. 145, for Coast Steamships, Adelaide. 28/04/1925: She left Greenock, but only reached Adelaide on 19 August. The Blue Funnel *Theseus* towed her to Padang after losing all the propeller blades after leaving Colombo. 24/08/1960: To Soc. Maritime du Pacifique Port Vila, renamed *Aldebaran*. 25/04/1966: Wrecked at Goro, New Caledonia. (D. Brown)

1Sc-MV **SAINT BLANE**
23/06/1955: James Lamont & Co., Port Glasgow, yard no. 383, for J. & A. Gardner & Co. Ltd. 12/09/1979: Arrived at Suez for scrapping, started breaking August 1979, completed April 1980. Previous names: *Gulf Planet* (1971); *Zuhair* (1976). (Author)

PS **LA MARGUERITE**
23/04/1894: Fairfield, Govan, yard no. 375, for Palace Steamers, managed by Victoria Steamboat Association. Was repossessed by builders. On cross-Channel and excursion routes. 1904: To Liverpool & North Wales SS Co. Liverpool. Requisitioned as a transport ship in WWI. One season under charter by IOMSP in 1919. 1925: Scrapped by T.M. Ward at Briton Ferry. (Author's collection)

2Sc-MV **LOCHMOR**
11/06/1989: Ailsa Shipbuilding Co., Troon, yard no. 554, for Caledonian MacBrayne's Small Islands service from Mallaig, with a summer capacity for 120 passengers and 2 cars. 2001: Sold to Landwest Corp., Campbeltown, then to R.J. Grant, New Milton. 2003: To Brixham Belle Cruises, Paignton. Later names: *Loch Awe*, *Torbay Belle* and *Jurassic Scene* of Blue Line Cruises from 2009. (Author)

2Sc-MV **MAID OF ARGYLL**
04/03/1953: A. & J. Inglis, Pointhouse, Glasgow, yard no. 1491P, for Caledonian Steam Packet Co. A Maid class ferry – last in service. 01/03/1974: To Greece and altered with additional decks and used for day trips to Corfu, Poros and Hydra. Renamed *City of Piraeus*, *City of Hydra* and *City of Corfu*. 14/05/1997: Damaged by fire at Corfu and sank at her berth. (Author)

2Sc-ST **MAID OF ORLEANS**
17/09/1948: William Denny & Bros, Dumbarton, yard no. 1414, for British Transport Commission, Southern Region. Initially for Folkestone–Boulogne route, later Dover–Calais service. First short sea vessel fitted with Denny Brown stabilisers. She could carry 1,400 passengers and 30 cars loaded by crane to after hold in winter only. 09/1975: Laid up at Newhaven. 06/11/1975: Left Newhaven for scrapping at Santander. (A. Duncan, *Ships in Focus*)

1Sc-2Cyl **OAK**
20/09/1906: John Fullerton & Co., Paisley, yard no. 191, for Joseph Fisher & Co., Newry. Her outfit was somewhat basic with a 2-cylinder compound reciprocating engine and use of a cargo winch and lead to handle mooring ropes and the anchor cable. 15/09/1951: Arrived for scrapping at Llanelli. (WSSPL)

2Sc-MV **PACIFIC COAST**
09/01/1947: Ardrossan Dockyard, yard no. 403, for Coast Lines. Renamed *Kuwait Coast* (1968); *Mohamed Nasser* (1974); *Nassar* (1975). 29/11/1976: Grounded on a breakwater at Port Rashid, Dubai. 09/1977: The wreck was taken and dumped outside the harbour. (B. Fielden, J. & M. Clarkson)

1Sc-T3Cyl **PLADDA (III)**
04/10/1907: Scotts' of Greenock, yard no. 421, for Clyde Shipping Co.'s Irish Sea Trades. 06/01/1917: Requisitioned by Admiralty as armed decoy ship Q.24, alias *Laggan*. 10/02/1936: Sold to Belfast, Mersey & Manchester Steamship Co. Ltd, Liverpool. 19/03/1936: Renamed *Mountstewart*. 30/12/1949: Arrived at Preston for scrapping by T.M. Ward. 09/03/1950: Breaking up started. (Author's collection)

3Sc-ST **QUEEN MARY II**
30/03/1933: William Denny & Bros, Dumbarton, yard no. 1262, for Williamson-Buchanan Steamers Ltd. Originally on Glasgow–Clyde coast run. Originally coal fired with two funnels, but converted to oil and one larger funnel fitted in 1957. 1935: To CSP. Final days with Caledonian MacBrayne. Converted to floating restaurant in London in 1981, prepared for tow to France, now docked at Tilbury. (Author)

2Sc-MV **REBORN**
1886: Robert Duncan & Co. Ltd, Port Glasgow, as *Cicciolina*. Renamed *Cerboli* in 1980 and name as shown in 1982 and seen at Malta in 1985. New S.A. Ansaldo manufactured engines installed in 1947; probably a steam ship originally, given date of construction. (Author)

1-Sc-MV **RENGANG**
1923: George Brown & Co., Greenock, yard no. 142, for Straits Steamship Co., Penang. Designed by J. Pollock. Assembled by builders and shipped in pieces for re-assembly by owners at Sungai Nyok (yard no. 22).
11/01/1942: Abandoned at Penang and taken by Japanese. No further record of eventual fate. (D. Brown)

1Sc-MV **ROMPIN**
1924: George Brown & Co., Greenock, yard no. 144, for Straits Steamship Co., Penang. Designed by J. Pollock. Assembled by builders and shipped in pieces for re-assembly by owners at Sungai Nyok. 15/02/1942: Captured by Japanese at Muntok after engine broke down. 09/1945: Found at Singapore in a stripped condition and subsequently broken up. (D. Brown)

2Sc-MV **ROYAL DAFFODIL II**
06/12/1957: James Lamont & Co., Port Glasgow, yard no. 391, for Wallasey Local Government Board. 1977: To Greek owners, lengthened and converted to a passenger RO/RO and container ship. 11/2007: Sank 20 miles off Cape Andreas, Cyprus (captain and first mate lost). Other names were: *Royal Daffodil* (1968); *Ioulis Keas II* (1977); *Agia Kyriaki* (1992); *Dolphin I* (1994). (Author's collection)

1Sc-TC3yl **SARDIS**
14/02/1928: Ardrossan Dockyard, yard no. 339, for J. & P. Hutchison, later Moss Hutchison. Later names: *Marichu* (1954); *Phloisvos* (1965); *Capo Pala* (1965); *Agios Nicolaos* (1967). 04/1969: Scrapped at Piraeus. (Roy Fenton)

3Sc-ST **SNAEFELL**
10/03/1906: Fairfield, Govan, yard no. 444, as *Viper* for G. & J. Burns Ltd, Glasgow, for their daylight Ardrossan–Belfast service. 27/03/1920: To the IOM SP Co. Ltd, renamed *Snaefell* that June, and remained in service until 1945. To Port Glasgow breakers Smith & Houston in 1946 but not broken up until three years later. (B. Fielden, J. & M. Clarkson)

2Sc-VS **SOUND OF SANDA**
01/04/1938: William Denny & Bros, Dumbarton, yard no. 1322, as *Lymington*, for Southern Railway Co. Lymington–Yarmouth service. She was the first Voith Schneider-propelled vessel to enter service in the UK. 1955: New vertical units fitted. 25/03/1974: To Western Ferries and new ramps fitted to suit Hunter's Quay-McInroys Point route. 12/1993: To Oban owner; despite efforts for preservation was dismantled and abandoned in Loch Etive near Oban. (Author)

2Sc-MV **SOUTHSEA**
11/03/1948: William Denny & Bros, Dumbarton, yard no. 1411, for British Transport Commission Southern Region. Ran on Portsmouth–Ryde, Isle of Wight for 38 years; thereafter went through a succession of different owners. 09/1987: Chartered by Waverley Excursions for Clyde cruising. 04/04/2005: Scrapped at Esbjerg. (Author)

2Sc-MV **ST TRILLO**
24/03/1936: Fairfield, Govan, yard no. 657, as *St Silio* for the Liverpool & North Wales Steamship Co. Ltd. She was renamed *St Trillo* in 1945 and had a number of owners since 1962. She later operated for a period on the Bristol Channel before being laid up for a few years. 21/04/1975: Finally towed from Barry to Dublin for scrapping. (Malcolm Cranfield)

DEP **TALISMAN**
10/04/1935: A. & J. Inglis, Pointhouse, Glasgow, yard no. 956, for London & North Eastern Railway. First diesel electric paddler in the world. 08/1940: Requisitioned and converted to AA ship HMS *Aristocrat* in 1940; in five years' service covered 46,583 miles. 07/1946: Back in service after refit. 1951: Transferred to CSP. 1954: Re-engined. 17/10/1967: Towed to Dalmuir for scrapping. (Author)

1Sc-T3Cyl **THORN**
31/05/1934: Scott & Sons, Bowling, yard no. 326, for same owners as *Oak* (Joseph Fisher & Co., Newry).
1954: Sold to Hay & Co., Lerwick, and managed by W.N. Lindsay of Leith and renamed *Colombine*.
24/12/1957: On passage from Baltasound, Unst, to Middlesbrough, stranded off Peterhead and later broken up. (WSSPL)

5

PUFFERS

A type ever associated with the Clyde and West Highlands, gaining an exaggerated romanticism given its rather mundane duties and appointments, was the puffer. Yet its importance in providing a lifeline to the subsistence of the many small and remote settlements relatively inaccessible by road cannot be denied. Initially designed to suit the limits of the Forth & Clyde and Crinan Canals, larger vessels were introduced which were denied these scenic and picturesque traverses. But even with the introduction of motor-driven coasters by the owners, the name puffer continued to be applied.

1Sc-2Cyl **ARDFERN**
1910: Peter McGregor, Kirkintilloch, order no. 129527, for T. Dougall and R. Stirrat of Glasgow. She was later owned by Warnock Brothers of Paisley, dredging and carrying sand and gravel. 1966: Scrapped at Dalmuir. (Author)

1Sc-2Cyl **CUMBRAE LASS**
1923: Scott & Sons, Bowling, yard no. 293, as *Pibroch* and transported coal and barley to Lagavulin Distillery on Islay. 1957: Replaced by motor vessel; sold to D. MacCorkindale of Troon, renamed *Texa*, then to A. McNeill of Greenock and later to Burke, renamed *Cumbrae Lass*. Later took rubbish from US Polaris base ship in the Holy Loch. 1967: Scrapped by Arnott & Young at Dalmuir. (Author)

1Sc-2Cyl **GLENHOLM**
26/08/1930: Scott & Sons, Bowling, yard no. 319, as *Glencloy* (III) for G. & G. Hamilton. 1955: She was converted to oil firing and fitted with wheelhouse forward of shortened funnel. 1966: To Alexander McNeil of Greenock, renamed *Glenholm*. 1967: Stranded at Cove in Loch Long and broken up. (Author)

1Sc-2Cyl **INCA**
1938: J. & J. Hay Ltd, Kirkintilloch, order no. 165958, for own use. Similar to the 1941-built *Boer*. 1965: Scrapped. (Edward Paget-Tomlinson)

1Sc-MV **KAFFIR (II)**
1944: J. & J. Hay Ltd, Kirkintilloch, yard no. 61, for J. Hay & Sons. Ordered as a VIC-type puffer, one of two built in Scotland, but cancelled and named *Kaffir*; the other, VIC18, renamed *Spartan*. 1962: Re-engined with a diesel. 23/09/1974: Lost in somewhat mysterious circumstances with her engineer aboard; stranded on Newton Beach off the port of Ayr and wrecked. (Author)

1Sc-MV **LASCAR**
1939: Scott & Sons, Bowling, yard no. 353, for J. Hay & Sons. With *Kaffir*, had deeper stern and wider hatch, and was to be forerunner of numerous VIC craft. Four steam and nine motor of 66ft class were built, and only two were built in Scotland, VIC18 and *Kaffir*. 1958: Re-engined. (Author)

1Sc-2Cyl **MELLITE**
1886: Murdoch & Murray, Port Glasgow, yard no. 95, as iron barge *Salisbury*. 1880: Bought by Ross & Marshall, who installed a Plenty compound engine. She was used as a water carrier in WWI and WWII. 1960s: Carried mail and luggage to Cunard and CPS liners at the Tail of the Bank. 1968: Scrapped at Dalmuir, still with original engine. (Author)

1Sc-MV **RAYLIGHT**
03/09/1963: Scotts' of Greenock, yard no. 695, for Ross & Marshall. A modern development of the original puffers. 04/08/1975: Sank, en route from Skye to Kilroot to load salt, in about 10 minutes off Larne when struck the Highland Rocks in thick fog; fortunately crew were rescued by the ferry *Ulida*. She was followed in 1965 by the larger *Dawnlight* from same builders. (Author)

1Sc-2Cyl **STARLIGHT**
12/01/1937: Ferguson Bros, Port Glasgow, yard no. 312, for Ross & Marshall, who operated her all her life. Built to the 66ft limit to suit the locks on the Forth & Clyde Canal. Cost £4,000 when built. 1967: Broken up. Sister ship *Skylight* was converted to diesel; after lying derelict at Greenock was finally scrapped. (Author)

STARLIGHT
This excellent model will give a good impression of the deck layout of a typical puffer. This was built by Andrew Green of Canada, formerly Glasgow, to a model plan I drew for a model magazine some years ago. (Model by Andrew Green)

6

Tugs

The tug operators on the Clyde came to be dominated by the Clyde Shipping Company and Steel & Bennie, the first being formed in 1815 and the latter in 1856. In addition to the usual ship handling, tugs were necessary in the early days of shipping on the Clyde as the navigation of seagoing vessels effectively stopped at Port Glasgow, hence the name as it was then the port of Glasgow, and cargo was transhipped into barges and towed up to Glasgow. Later years saw takeovers and amalgamations which were to finally obliterate the characteristic colours of the two fleets.

1Sc-MV **BRIGADIER**
05/12/1960: George Brown & Co., Greenock, yard no. 273, for Steel & Bennie. Transferred to Cory Ship Towage (Clyde) Ltd. 1976: Renamed *Forager*. 1976: To Whitliff Corp. Ltd, renamed *Fortrose*. 1979: To Soc. Armamento Gestione Nav. S.a.r.L., Italy, still in service January 2000. (Author)

1Sc-MV **CAMPAIGNER**
30/07/1957: James Lamont & Co., Port Glasgow, yard no. 390, for Steel & Bennie. 1970: Transferred to Cory Ship Towage (Clyde) Ltd. 1977: To Frank Pierce (Tugs) Ltd. Renamed *Pulwell Victor*. 1981: Sold to Atrefs Shipping Co., Greece, renamed *Maranbu*. 1984: To Kappa Mar. Co., Greece, renamed *Kappa*. 23/08/2004: Scrapped at Aliaga, Turkey. (Author)

2Sc-VS **CARRICKFERGUS**
20/11/1975: Scott & Sons, Bowling, yard no. 452, as *Greatham Cross* for Tees Towing Co. Ltd, Middlesbrough. Fitted with two forward mounted azimuthing multi-directional propellers. 1990: Company acquired by Cory Towage (Tees) Ltd. 07/1994: Moved to Cory Towage, Belfast, and renamed *Carrickfergus*. Still in service at Aberdeen with sister *Cultra*, ex-*Skelton Cross*. (Author)

1Sc-MV **FLYING DRAKE**
29/11/1956: A. & J. Inglis, Pointhouse, Glasgow, yard no. 1570P, for Clyde Shipping Co.; sister to same builder's *Flying Duck*. 1969: Sold to Rimorchiatori Sardi S.p.A, Italy, renamed *Oristano*. (Author)

1Sc-MV **FLYING FOAM (IV)**
07/06/1962: Ferguson Bros, Port Glasgow, yard no. 435, for Clyde Shipping Co. 1981: Sold to Medit S.P.A., Italy, renamed *Nuvola Rossa.* 1977: Sold to Rimorchiatori Siciliani S.R.l., Italy. (Author)

1Sc-MV **FLYING SCOUT (II)**
23/07/1969: Scott & Sons, Bowling, yard no. 439, for Clyde Shipping Co. From 1986 to 1992 had several transfers within Ireland. 1992: Sold to Malcuth S.r.l, Italy, renamed *Adebaran*; towed to Palermo by *Alce Nero*, ex-*Flying Fulmar*. 05/1994: Sold to Rimorchiatori Siciliani, renamed *Leoncillo*. 09/2003: Scrapped. (Author)

PS **GEORGE BROWN**
11/01/1887: Samuel McKnight, Ayr, yard no. 10, for Irvine Harbour Board. Independently coupled paddles driven by two surface-condensing, direct-acting diagonal engines supplied by William Kemp of Glasgow. Last paddle tug on the Clyde, and possibly last in UK, when withdrawn early in 1957. 14/01/1957: Arrived at Troon towing the explosives ship *Lady Dorothy*, both to be broken up there. (Author's collection)

2Sc-T3cyl **J.R. MORE**
1961: Ferguson Bros, Port Glasgow, yard no. 431, for South African Railways. 29/07/1961: Entered service. Could be distinguished from her sister *F.C. Sturrock* by continuous line of bulwark top rail. *Danie Hugo* was last steam to be withdrawn in June 1984; was later moored next to a jetty at the Esplanade as a prize exhibit in the Durban Maritime Museum. (Author's collection)

1Sc-T3cyl **LAHEJ**
19/07/1927: Harland and Wolff, Greenock, yard no. 796, for P&O in service at Aden. Sold for scrap there in 1961 but reported still surviving in 1963. (Author)

2Sc-VS **TIRRICK** (Shetland term for Tern)
01/02/1983: Ferguson Bros, Port Glasgow, yard no. 489, for Shetland Tugs Ltd. This was a registered company set up with Clyde Shipping and Cory in October 1974 to operate tugs servicing tankers at the Sullom Voe oil terminal in Shetland, initially with Ferguson-built sister *Shalder* (oyster catcher). (Author's collection)

1Sc-MV **WARRIOR**
17/09/1935: Scott & Sons, Bowling, yard no. 332, for Steel & Bennie, Glasgow. 1958: Re-engined with a Widdop diesel engine. 1968: Sold to Falmouth Towage Co. Ltd and renamed *Agnes*. 01/08/1985: Scrapped. (Author)

7

Dredgers

Given that Glasgow as a port was relatively inaccessible in the early days, barges and scows initially had to be towed up over shallow banks taking advantage of the tide. The port's subsequent predominance was wholly dependent on the deepening of the River Clyde to cater for the ever-increasing size of ships. Thus it is not surprising that a number of dredge builders came to be established on the river, honing their skills building a range of dredgers to suit the different local conditions. The experience they gained ultimately resulted in them supplying numerous ports around the world.

1Sc-T3Cyl **ANADRIAN**
08/05/1952: Ferguson Bros, Port Glasgow, yard no. 402. Grab hopper dredger for Government of Malta. 03/07/1953: Left Greenock for delivery voyage. 1993: Hull broken up and much of the machinery and triple-expansion engine preserved in working order on show in a Malta museum. (Author)

2Sc-T3Cyl **ANNIE W. LEWIS**
28/06/1927: William Simons & Co., Renfrew, yard no. 683. Hopper suction dredger with suction pipe in stern tunnel for Aberdeen Harbour Commissioners. 09/1953: Underwent a special survey which included drilling for a check of some deck and shell plates. 1969: To Bakker en Zoon, Zeebrugge. 20/01/1970: Scrapped. (Author)

1Sc-T3cl **CESSNOCK**
08/04/1954: Fleming & Ferguson, Paisley, yard no. 770, for Clyde Navigation Trust. 15/01/1958: Dredger and a hopper moored at Princes Pier during storm. Torn from her moorings, she capsized with loss of 3 lives. 11/04/1968: Raised by W.A. van den Tak with salvage vessel *Bever* using polystyrene grains which were expanded to give lifting buoyancy under control of sheerlegs. 1974: Sold to Italy. (Author)

2Sc-T3Cyl **HOPPER NO. 25**
08/02/1954: W. Simons & Co. Ltd, Renfrew, yard no. 798, for Clyde Navigation Trust. Used with bucket dredger *Blythswood* to dredge for *QE2* launch. Leaky boiler tubes started to give problems when operating a five-day week from 1970, having to keep steam up on Saturdays and Sundays. 20/10/1983: Scrapped. (Author)

2-Sc-T3Cyl **LENNOX**
05/02/1954: Ferguson Bros, Port Glasgow, yard no. 406. Grab hopper dredger for Clyde Navigation Trust, later Clyde Port Ltd in 1965. 15/08/1983: Arrived at Manchester. 08/09/1983: Scrapped by Stretford Shipbreakers Ltd. (Author)

INCE
1976: Ferguson Bros, Port Glasgow, yard no. 472, for Manchester Ship Canal Co. Dumb bucket dredger, later sold to C.W. Shipping of County Clare, Ireland, and dredged the tidal River Barrow from New Ross downstream and the Suir in Waterford; also for the marina at Kilrush. Last seen laid up on mud near Inishmurray Pier on County Clare side of the Shannon Estuary. (Stephen Brown)

2Sc-DEMV **ONEZHSKIY**
10/11/1965: Alexander Stephen & Sons, Linthouse, yard no. 687. One of trio of suction dredgers built for USSR. 1,972grt and 272ft overall; was fitted with bow thruster with provision for dredging on either side. The suction pipe with flexible coupling can clearly be seen lying on deck, with suction connection above the fore end. (Author)

8

Miscellaneous

This chapter includes a selection which perhaps does not readily conform to the definitions previously described, but provides a snapshot of the skills of the Clyde shipbuilders, boatbuilders and engineers as epitomised by the variety of the types illustrated.

2Sc-MV **ABERTHAW FISHER**
18/02/1996: Ailsa Shipbuilding Co., yard no. 522. With Aberdeen-built *Kingsnorth Fisher*, designed for transporting heavy equipment for power stations, shipped on trailers via an adjustable ramp and on to an elevating platform to lower into the hold. 1990: Renamed *National Generator*. 1996: Renamed *Moonstar* after conversion to a diamond dredger working off Namibia. 2000: Scrapped in India. (WSSPL)

SV **ARCHIBALD RUSSELL**
23/01/1905: Scotts' of Greenock, yard no. 391. Steel four-masted barque for John Hardie & Co. Last square-rigged sailing ship of her class to be built in Britain. 03/01/1924: To Captain G. Eriksen. 06/1941: Detained by UK Government and used as grain store ship at Goole. 23/04/1947: Returned to owner, but offered for sale. 1949: Scrapped by J.J. King at Gateshead. (A. Duncan, *Ships in Focus*)

2Sc-SMV **BRENDA**
22/06/1951: William Denny & Bros, Dumbarton, yard no. 1453. Fishery protection patrol vessel for Department of Agriculture & Fisheries for Scotland. 08/1982: To Sociedad Naviera Lanaxa S.A., Pajama, renamed *Brenda S.* (Author)

2Sc-2Cyl **BUFFEL**
10/03/1868: Robert Napier, Govan, yard no. 139. Iron armoured monitor/ram ship for Royal Netherlands Navy for coastal defence duties; never saw any active service. Served for periods as training and accommodation ship. Original guns and engines removed; now preserved museum ship at the Prins Hendrik Maritiem Museum, Rotterdam. (Author)

MV CENTAUR & **SS BRITISH MARINER**
John Brown, Clydebank, showing MV *Centaur*, yard no. 722, and SS *British Mariner*, yard no. 717, fitting out in 1963. The prominent 150-ton cantilever crane on west side of fitting-out basin was supplied by Sir William Arrol in 1907. (Author)

SV **CUTTY SARK**
22/06/1869: Linton & Hope, Dumbarton, yard no. 5, a composite clipper for 'Old White Hat' John Willis of London but was finished by Denny's. Had moderate success as a tea clipper but as a wool clipper under Captain Woodget made fast passages. 1895: To Portugal, renamed *Fereirra*. 1916: Sold, renamed *Mario Do Amparo*. 1922: Bought by Captain Dowman who started restoration; now preserved at Greenwich. (Author's collection)

1Sc-DEMV **FAIRTRY II LH270**
27/01/1959: William Simons & Co., Renfrew, yard no. 808, for Christian Salvesen. Second of pioneering freezer stern factory trawlers. 1967: Laid up at Tonsberg. 10/1971: To Vickers Oceanics Ltd (James Fisher & Sons Ltd managers) as a mother ship for submersibles. 04/1972: Renamed *Vickers Voyager*. 06/1969: To British Oceanics Ltd, renamed *British Voyager*. 16/08/1984: Scrapping began at Troon. (A. Duncan, *Ships in Focus*)

2Sc-MV **GRACE PATERSON RITCHIE**
1965: Yarrow Shipbuilders Ltd, Glasgow, yard no. 2272, as 70ft Clyde class lifeboat no. 70-002 for RNLI. First steel RNLI boat; her £57,000 cost was met by legacy of Miss Grace Paterson Ritchie of Skelmorlie. She was sold to Iceland and renamed *Henry A. Halfdansson*. 2002: Bought by Iain Crosbie, renamed *Grace Ritchie* and has been much restored. (I. Crosbie)

1Sc-T4yl **GRETA**
21/04/1898: Scotts' of Greenock, yard no. 354, for John Scott IV. Scotts' built six yachts named *Greta* and one *Grainaig* for the family. Had numerous owners since 1900; not as a yacht since 1920. Owned by Epirotiki Steam Navigation Co., Piraeus. 23/04/1941: Bombed and sunk. This model was built to my model plan and was an exhibition award winner for Don Brown. (Author's collection)

1Sc-2Cyl-AUX **HINEMOA**
07/05/1876: Scotts' of Greenock, yard no. 172, for New Zealand Government. Used as lighthouse tender and survey ship. 1907: Rescued the survivors of sailing vessel *Dundonald* wrecked off Auckland Island. 1929: Sold to D.W. Mackay of Invercargill and used as tourist ship. 1932: Laid up and stripped of gear. 1944: Towed out for target shelling practice; sunk by demolition charge. Builder's plate presented to shipbuilders. (Author's collection)

2Sc-DEMV **OCEAN SEEKER**
25/02/1970: Ferguson Bros, Port Glasgow, yard no. 457, for Commissioners of Irish Lights tender *Granuaile*. Introduced passive anti-roll tank, helicopter deck and VP propeller to fleet; bow thruster and buoy-handling crane fitted later. Suffix (II) added to allow replacement vessel being built in Holland to take her name. 17/02/2002: Withdrawn from service and bought by Gardline Shipping of Yarmouth for hydrographic duties, renamed *Ocean Seeker*. (Author)

1Sc-MV **PROSPECTOR BA25**
1973: Alexander Noble & Sons, Girvan, yard no. 73. One of the handsome wooden fishing boats built at this yard, proudly displaying the Scottish thistle carved on her name board. She was a successful fisher and the only transom-sterned ring netter built. Later port numbers were: SH2 (1983); TT25 (1991); N1 (2006). Seen here going on trials. (J.H. Murray)

2Sc-SS **SALFORD CITY**
28/06/1928: William Beardmore & Co., Dalmuir, yard no. 652, for operation between Davyhulme on the Manchester Ship Canal and open water as a sludge vessel. She was fitted with twin diesels in 1963 and underwent a rebuild which included a new funnel. 24/06/1997: Arrived at Fleetwood after continuous service; scrapped by Mayer, Newman & Co. (Author)

2Sc-2Cyl **TORCH**
16/05/1924: Ailsa Shipbuilding Co., Ayr, yard no. 387, for Trustees of Clyde Lighthouses as a buoy lighthouse/buoy tender. Based at Port Glasgow until the trustees' workshops were transferred to Victoria Harbour, Greenock. 1965: To Clyde Port Authority. Original steam crane replaced by hydraulically powered speed crane derrick. 1980: Sold for scrapping at Dalmuir. Replaced by converted coaster *River Avoca*, renamed *Torch*. (Author)

2Sc-MV **VIGILANT (III)**
03/12/1935: William Denny & Bros, Dumbarton, yard no. 1280, as fishery protection vessel. Original appearance superficially designed to represent a trawler. 08/1939: Requisitioned as examination vessel on Clyde. 04/1943: Renamed *Ixion*. 04/1946: Returned to department and resumed service in 1947. 1980: Renamed *Vigilant II*. 03/1983: To Sheridan Trading Inc. S.A., Panama, renamed *Vigilant*; fate unknown. (Author)

MANIPUR (III)
A typical scene taken from the bridge when steaming up the Red Sea in March 1959; one of three voyages on this ship. 06/01/1967: Arrived at Whampoa for scrapping. (Author)

The former Scotts' of Greenock dry dock at Cartsburn. This was constructed by the builders *c.* 1800; previously they had to take their turn at the municipally owned dry dock which was built in 1786. Following the demolition of Scotts' shipyard the dry dock was left abandoned, with entrance blocked off as seen: a lamentable and the only tangible reminder of over 250 years of shipbuilding. (Author)

The wooden bridge structure, open steam winches and tall funnel exemplified by the Brocklebank doyen of 1917 SS *Maihar* (I); still smart in 1958. (Author)

In contrast is the complex steel bridge front, bipod masts, domed funnel and enclosed steam winches of the same company's 1957-built ship SS *Masirah* (II). (Author)

If you enjoyed this book, you may also be interested in…

HM Naval Base Clyde

KEITH HALL

978 0 7524 6480 0

Wooden Fishing Boats of Scotland

JAMES A. POTTINGER

978 0 7524 8757 1

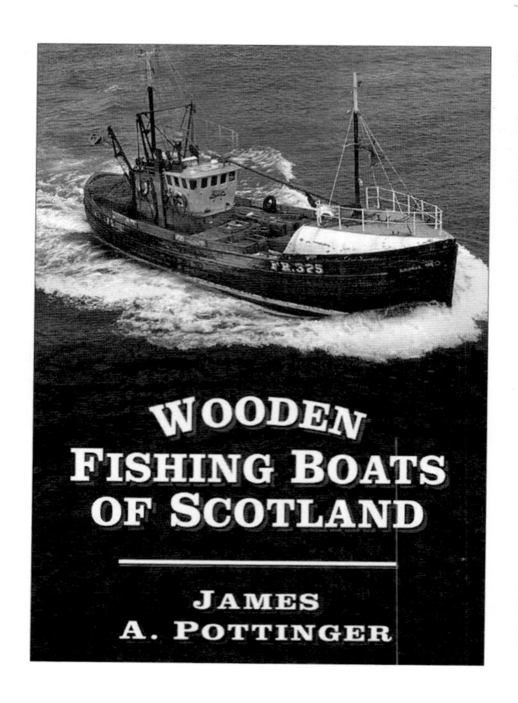